ORGANISING LOCAL EVENTS

BY SARAH PASSINGHAM

published by THE DIRECTORY OF SOCIAL CHANGE

in association with THE INSTITUTE OF CHARITY FUNDRAISING MANAGERS

ORGANISING LOCAL EVENTS

by
Sarah Passingham

Published by The Directory of Social Change

Copyright © 1993 Sarah Passingham

BRITISH LIBRARY CATALOGUING-IN-PUBLICATION DATA
A catalogue record for this book is available from the British Library

ISBN 1 873860 10 2

Typeset by Linda Parker

Printed and bound by Page Bros., Norwich

CONTENTS

ACKNOWLEDGEMENTS

There are many chapters in this book that have had an input from a variety of sources and I should like to thank all those who have given facts and opinions so freely. In particular I should like to thank Duncan Smith, Principal Environmental Health Officer for Norwich for his help and advice for the chapter on Food and Andrew Smiley, director of Shell Shock Fireworks for editing the chapter on Fireworks. I am also very grateful to Phil Norton and Owen Warnock from Eversheds, Norwich who have advised me and checked the legal information contained in Chapters 16 and 25.

Norwich City Council also deserve a mention in this section. Through a sensitive and thorough provision of leisure for the citizens of the City of Norwich, an environment has been created in which I have been able to develop my skills in devising, organising and funding a wide variety of events. I should like to thank my first Norwich boss, Paul Jelley, for giving me this valuable opportunity.

With grateful thanks also, to my husband Dennis who spent many hours editing and re-editing the text.

INTRODUCTION

I have had a lot of fun from running events and shows; it has been hard work but I have always done it in the knowledge that I was being paid for my many hours toil. There are hundreds, probably thousands of volunteers who work just as hard for no financial remuneration at all and I have enormous admiration for them. I have worked with a good many Lions, Rotarians, Scouts and Guides and even individuals who have had a burning ambition to do something for a particular community and they are always good humoured and enthusiastic even in the face of adversity. When things go wrong it is desperately disappointing and disheartening. Perhaps by looking at some of my suggestions and learning from my mistakes most of those disappointing times can be averted.

This guide is not meant as the definitive work on organising events, but rather as some scaffolding on which to hang your own ideas and methods of doing things.

I am not a lawyer, neither am I an accountant so for complicated or particular problems relating to these areas it is always worth bringing in specialist knowledge. Individual circumstances will vary with every event but I hope to give you the basic legal requirements or at least set some alarm bells ringing where necessary.

To borrow the first words from another guide - 'DON'T PANIC'. Events grow like Topsy and I have myself come close to falling apart on occasions but it achieved nothing and did not inspire my colleagues. I hope this book will act as a buffer - to be used before you go off the rails! - and to allow you not only to appear calm and well organised but to know that you are.

I still use an excellent piece of advice given to me by my first Local Authority boss - Roger Dyason, now Director of the Free Trade Hall, Manchester - 'It tends not to matter what decision you make as long as you make it early enough and stick to it'. I'd like to add a rider to that statement, 'make sure that the people you are working with know what that decision is!' In nearly 10 years of working with every type of professional and amateur, indoors and out, and where plans have moved from a to b and sometimes to c due to bad weather, illness, mistake or other reasons too numerous to mention, I don't think that the general public have ever realised what was going on behind the scenes. Sometimes what they were experiencing was far removed from the original concept but nobody minded and more often than not, nobody knew.

People always go to an event prepared to enjoy themselves and I have often thought how lucky I am to be able to work in a happy atmosphere and to be outside for a large proportion of the summer months.

I hope that with a little help from this guide your fetes, fairs and shows will be trouble free and that you will have time to enjoy them as well as achieving your objectives, be that making money for your cause or bringing a little sunshine into the lives of those less fortunate than ourselves.

Good luck and have fun.

Sarah Passingham
February 1993

1 OBJECTIVES

Before going any further have you thought through what it is you are trying to achieve? Sometimes you may decide on two or more objectives, but it is a good idea to put these in order of priority: work it out on paper if it helps you to clarify your thoughts.

All organisers for charity events will at least wish to cover their expenses and most will put fundraising as their main objective. A community event may not be so concerned with raising cash as bringing together different sections of an area, celebrating a specific date or just all getting together to give the rest of the neighbourhood a good time.

Sometimes something more specific is in mind such as raising the level of awareness for some previously generally unknown service or activity. This sort of event is often more of an exhibition and frequently is of an educative nature. Many events are a mixture of all of these.

At this point I should like to start telling you the story of a special but not untypical individual. It is not the true confessions of Bill Pincher - 'Events Organiser Extraordinaire'. It is a product of my imagination but serves as a good example of how many events start and develop. It might help you to see how some decisions and thought processes work.

Bill's story starts overleaf. He works for the RSPCA and is proposing to organise an event on a housing estate. He starts by setting out his priorities.

Having made his list and sorted out the priorities, Bill is now in a position to start matching his objectives to ideas. At this stage he might include other people to help in the decision process. (See Chapter 4 on Committees).

KEY POINTS

1 Work out your objectives before you decide on an event.

2 Decide on your priorities.

3 Decide if you will bring in help in the form of a committee or if you will 'go it alone'.

4 Match your priorities to the different elements.

▶▶ BILL'S PROGRESS

Bill Pincher works for the RSPCA in a large town. He is concerned for the way that dogs are used as presents during the Christmas period and the high numbers that are later abandoned or cruelly treated by families who didn't realise that the puppy would grow so big or eat so much. He rightly surmises that ignorance is the main cause and wishes to make homes more dog-friendly. Bill knows of one large housing estate which is rather run-down but the people are lively and community-minded, although sometimes not seeing quite eye-to-eye with the local police, and he would like to give them an opportunity for a bit of fun. The RSPCA could do with a bit of extra in the kitty also.

Bill might arrange his priorities something like this:

1. Raise level of awareness about the needs of dogs

2. Break even on expenses

3. Involve the inhabitants of the estate

4. Put on a 'bit-of-a-do' for those who do not usually go out for their entertainment

5. Make some money for the RSPCA

6. Help community relations between the estate and the local Police force

7. Get some personal satisfaction and enjoyment out of organising an event

2 IDEAS

In this chapter you will find a list of shows and events that you might like to consider. There are many, many more ideas than just those listed. Be creative, get your local community to tell you what they would like. I have had a go at most of the ideas on the list, and some are a lot harder work than others.

Which members of the community are you keen to involve? Some events fall naturally into one category or another. For instance you would not expect a needlework and knitting marathon to attract many men or children. Conversely a specialist athletics meeting will be largely confined to the under 25s. However, the village fair is bound to be a full scale family affair.

Most specialist events will suggest their own target group or, looking at the problem from the other direction, many specific groups will only be interested in a narrow band of events. See Chapter 6 for more information on target groups.

Often, and this is particularly true of fundraising events, you may be working to a brief that is as simple as 'to raise as much money as we can from as many people as we can attract': and that usually means a family event.

It is hard to devise events that involve all members of the family, but it is often greatly appreciated - nothing is more trying on a hot afternoon than attempting to enjoy a 'Family Fayre' with a bored toddler. Make sure those who are not so good on their feet have something to do where they can sit down even if it is only a nice spacious tea-tent. At the risk of gender-stereotyping, give Dad a chance to show off at the coconut shy or Mum an opportunity to buy someone else's cooking. Above all keep it condensed: it is better to have eight activities packed into two hours than six dragged out over four. Children and many adults will not wait long for the next attraction and your audience will start to drift away if they sense that the next event on the programme is not just around the corner.

Do not be deceived, community events are not the easy option despite being without the pressure of having to raise money; it can be as difficult getting people to part with their time as their money and you will have a great deal more work in the preliminary stages, although with more enthusiastic volunteers available by the time the big day arrives you may well have less to do at the end.

KEY POINTS

1 Make a considered choice of event and think of the specific groups that you may wish to attract.

2 Pack several elements into a short space of time rather than being tempted to spin things out, but make the various parts relevant to each other

3 Try to get a chance to study other events at first hand

In general if you get trade stand owners involved you will make more money than by working just with volunteers, but you must be professional: they are trying to run a business and the tolerance levels are lower. If you want a relaxed, gentle event, leave them out.

When you have decided on the size and 'feel' of your event, stick to your original plans and work off the objectives list like Bill Pincher in the previous chapter. By all means mix elements together, but only if they are relevant and try not to get too carried away. Fragmented shows are hard to organise, even harder to market and the public likes to know what it is getting.

Above all, the best piece of advice I can give is: having decided on an idea, go and see as many similar shows as you possibly can; observe the good points so that you can copy them. Decide why certain ideas irritate or confuse you. Have a good look at the structure of a site and how the organisers manage the signing or the parking of cars. If you are interested in making money study the ways that the public are parted from their cash and where the largest crowds are, even at what times of the day it seems to be most popular. You can read a guide from front to back, again and again but there is nothing so informative as going to look for yourself.

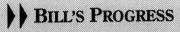

▶▶ BILL'S PROGRESS

Having made his list of objectives, Bill now tries to decide what elements are going to be right for the community that he has chosen to benefit from his event. He needs to include his 'message' within the framework of good entertainment. The sort of activities that Bill decides on are as follows:

1. Static exhibition of dog-care, different breeds, diseases, some shock pictures of what happens when there are problems, and a film show. These are the nub of the Dog Day and on their own would present a pretty boring show, so Bill has to dress it up a bit and encourage the public to see what he wants them to see by providing something that they will enjoy.

2. He intends to let out some stall spaces to pet shop owners, feed suppliers, local artists and crafts people and 'fast food' wagons etc. These will cover the expenses incurred from hiring the hall, printing the programmes, advertising and so on.

3. He thinks that the local school might agree to encourage children and parents to make costumes and masks for a parade to walk around the streets to drum up a crowd before the official start time.

4. The main activity will be a lighthearted dog show for the pets of the local community to be judged by a senior Officer of the local RSPCA. Between classes local bands, dancers, jugglers etc. will entertain the audience. Nearby, but in another area dog professionals and their dogs will be permanently available or on show.

5. A programme of the activities will be on sale with all proceeds going to the RSPCA. Each programme will have a lucky number for a prize draw at the end. The prize is donated by a local business in return for having the company name on the programme.

6. Bill has a dog-handler friend in the Police force, who agrees to bring some dogs and put on a demonstration of Police dog training and afterwards allow the public to see the dogs close to and answer questions.

7. If the day is properly organised and Bill doesn't get carried away by his own enthusiasm and manages to keep the show to a scale that suits the venue and the public, satisfaction of a job well done is guaranteed.

Here's the list of ideas for you to consider - mix them up, match them to others, think creatively and remember that you can always take things out, it is harder to keep adding: but try to keep to a theme.

Fete

Fair

Jumble sale

Themed Market

Barbecue

Cream teas

Highland Games

Sponsored Walk / Swim / Bike-ride / Hack etc.

Talent Competition

Olde Tyme Music Hall

Pantomime

Cabaret

Wine and Cheese evening

Exhibition, Art / Flower Arranging / Craft etc.

Dance Competition

Pet Show

Dog Show

Horse Show

Street Procession

Demonstration, Yoga / Painting / Cookery / Beauty etc.

Pop Concert

Dinner Dance

Open House and Garden Day

Car Rally

Treasure Hunt

Conker Competition

Go-Kart Races

Local Business Exhibition

Garden Produce Show

Magic Show

.Children's Day

Gymkhana

Fast Party (People pay not to attend)!

Raffle

Hoe Down

Roller Marathon

Fashion Show

Bonfire and Firework Display

Promise Auction

Book Sale

Antique Fair

Dutch Auction

Sports Meetings

Car Wash

Baby Show and

Glamourous Granny Competition

Balloon Race

Bring and Buy Sale

Strawberry Teas

Car Boot Sale

Carol Marathon

Teddy Bear's Picnic

Christmas Fair

Clay Pigeon Shoot
Bed Pushing
Coffee Morning
Bedlam Day for the Under 5s
Donkey Derby
Football Match
Cricket Match
Petanque Competition
Fun Run
Fortune Telling and Horoscope Day
Zodiac and Astrology Show
Hallowe'en Party
Demolition Derby
Stock Car Racing
Three-Wheeler Rally
Disco
Guided Walk
Film Show
Fun Fair
Carnival
Mini Golf Tournament
Model Makers Show
Home Produce Fair
Snow Party
Bygones and Agricultural Show
Heavy Horse Show
Tractor Display

Musical Recital
Puppet Show
Village Hall Quiz
Rag Week
Scavenger Hunt
Reel Party
Swimming Gala
Tennis Tournament
Sports for the Blind Display
Come and Try it Day
Toy Fair
Tug of War
Splurge Gun Games
Wine Tasting Evening
Its a Knockout Competition
Vintage Car Rally
Spine-chiller Trail
Celebrity Auction
Orienteering Day
Fancy Dress Party and Competition
Table Games Evening
Medieval Banquet
Specific event or date Celebration
Midsummer Ball
Regatta
Water Frolic
Tea Dance

3 WHEN AND WHERE?

In this chapter we will look at the things that govern possibly the most important decisions of all when holding an event.

There are many factors and alternatives to take into consideration when deciding when and where to hold an event. Sometimes the nature of the event means that some of these deliberations are already a 'fait accompli', due to an event traditionally being held on the Summer Bank Holiday weekend or perhaps because you have chosen a Midsummer Ball as your fundraising idea. Sometimes your choice of dates is limited for a chosen hall or park - you might find that Village Halls and Function Rooms are often booked years in advance for popular dates. Try not to compromise your event by taking second best. If you have planned for your Midsummer Party to be around the middle of June don't settle for May. If you expect 70 cars and 3,000 people to turn up for a Vintage Car Weekend don't agree on the local Recreation Ground if the City Park is unavailable.

CHOOSING A DATE

In choosing a date, think about the time of year. Weather is important not only for an outside event; people don't want to turn out in freezing conditions to then sit in a draughty church hall for 2 hours to listen to a Carol Concert or go on a boiling hot afternoon to a hall with no ventilation to see a film.

Consider an appropriate time of the year and time of day for your show - we have already talked about the more obvious midsummer parties - but don't forget the problem of long daylight hours if you plan to hold a 'son et lumiere' for instance or a firework display for school children, especially in the north of the country.

Meal times are worth consideration particularly where families are expected. Fetes and Fairs are generally busiest between 2pm and 4.30pm, i.e. between lunch and tea. Of course you can open in the mornings and you will catch a different crowd but it might be a good idea to save your most spectacular attractions for the afternoon.

School holidays may be important to you and these dates are available a year in advance from your local Education Authority.

KEY POINTS

To chose a date remember:

1. Probable weather conditions

2. Conditions of site or hall associated with the time of year

3. Traditions

4. Other local events in competition

5. Major national events e.g. Football, Wimbledon, Elections or even popular TV programmes

6. School Holidays

7. Specialist organisation advice

NOT TREADING ON TOES

Make sure no other organisation is having a similar event on the same date in your catchment area. If you live in a remote community any event may prove to be competition. You can check for conflicting shows with the local Tourist Information Centres, listings in your nearest library or by ringing your local Radio station. If you are holding a specialised event like a Horse Show then other horse and pony clubs or groups may well be able to help.

One other suggestion; it is always worth checking the television schedules if at all possible. I remember one fateful evening when I had booked a famous Russian pianist to play an equally famous programme and confidently waited for the 'Sold Out' sign to go up. Only 26 people turned up. I had forgotten that it was the final of the Leeds Piano Competition and my audience were at home watching their televisions. These sort of coincidences are hard to foretell, but the final of the FA Cup is published well in advance!

Make sure that all the important equipment you need is available for that date before you firm up on a day, including mobile loos, crowd barriers, marquees etc. Similarly, fields or some other space for car parking must be available, (after harvest in the country is always a good bet).

CHOOSING A VENUE

If finding the right date is difficult, getting the right venue may be easier. Often there is only one obvious choice and if this is not available you might do better to go back to basics and choose a different event or wait a while. If you have a smallish event you could do worse than to borrow a large back garden or front meadow and save your money rather than hiring the school sports field.

An inside event usually has to take place in a public hall, but you might find a sympathetic farmer or business-person to lend you a barn or warehouse. You may even find you could use a church for something appropriate. I have used marquees even in winter as an option, and provided that there are no gale-force winds and you use plenty of modern hot-air heaters they can be very successful. It is worth negotiating a good rate for a winter hire of marquees and you can often get them at short notice as they are usually readily available from October to March.

● ● ● ● ● ● ● ● ● ● ●

KEY POINTS

To chose a venue remember:

❶ Suit the site to the event

❷ Car parking availability

❸ Access

❹ Availability of facilities

❺ Try unusual venues

❻ Safety

❼ Neighbours

❽ Check licences if necessary

❾ Check local bylaws

Why not consider some more outlandish venues, such as the City's main street (a lot of negotiations needed here!) or on a boat or a steam train if you have a revived railway near you. You could even try putting something traditionally held indoors outside in a field or on the beach, such as a sculpture exhibition or a dance workshop.

Some town councils are prepared to let empty office space or shops for a limited period if they are sympathetic to the cause. Ask the Local Authority Estates Officer or Planning Officer well in advance as you may need temporary Planning Permission for Change of Use.

More prosaic factors to keep in mind are whether public loos are available or do you need to hire mobiles. Space to park cars is vital unless an event is very small and you only expect people on foot. Have you suitable access for disabled people - or mothers with pushchairs? Do you need water, electricity or gas? Some parks have all-weather electrical points and may even be able to provide a three phase supply if necessary; it is always worth asking. If your event is staged you may need a building with a lighting rig or at the very least a structure that is capable of taking one. Again for a staged performance you might need blackout facilities and dressing rooms. Even shade for animals or whether the grass will need mowing before the big day might need consideration.

Check local bylaws. You may have exceeded the number of days that entertainment can be held on a particular site, for instance. And you most certainly will not be able to hold an event on public land or in a building where safety is thought to be low or where neighbours run the risk of being disturbed.

Finally remember your caterers. They may seem the most picky and demanding of all your hired hands but they are responsible for people's health and governed by strict Hygiene Laws which mean that they could be closed down or prevented from working at your event if they do not comply with statutory guidelines. If you are planning to feed the public in any way other than just tea and a biscuit please read Chapter 25 carefully.

Most of the above can be provided on any site, be it permanent or hired in. Your biggest problem may be access - it is no good having everything ready to bring onto a park if the only way in is up a narrow lane between two rows of houses that you cannot even squeeze a car through. Having said that, some parks or recreation grounds with seemingly tiny gates have a removable section of fencing and the groundsmen are quite used to making a second entrance for vehicles.

Indoors might well have better facilities, especially if it is a licensed public building. The secret is not to be afraid to ask if you don't see what you need. I have usually found managers or officers to be most helpful as long as I have made it clear that I feel it is a favour they are doing me and not my God-given right. After all you are the one who is breezing in and about to turn their peaceful, easily run venue upside down!

 ## BILL'S PROGRESS

Arthur Pint and Bill go back a long way. In fact Arthur and Bill sat next to each other in school and now Arthur is married to Bill's sister, Molly. Together they run the 'Bowl and Whistle', a small tied pub in the Brick Close area. Over a lunch-time drink with Arthur, Bill explains his idea and after closing time they go to look for an open space that might be suitable.

They have three areas to chose from: the school sports field, the recreation ground next to a small community centre and the road and surrounding verges that goes right through the middle of the estate itself.

They swiftly reject the road as this is Bill's first effort in organising an event and he doesn't want to get involved in closing off highways.

They like the sports field, but it is rather large and separate from the estate. It does, however, solve the problem of where to park cars.

After Arthur points out that the only cars they can reasonably expect are those belonging to the organisers and stall holders, they agree to compromise. After all most of the visitors will be from the immediate and surrounding areas. They decide to ask the council if they can use the recreation ground and the community centre. They will also enquire if they can park cars on the school playground as it backs onto the community centre.

4 COMMITTEE OR 'GO IT ALONE'?

FOR AND AGAINST

I am always tempted to operate as a 'one-man-band', but even if you have unlimited spare time and resources to set the event up, it is almost impossible to organise the day itself with only one person. You physically cannot be in two or more places at once or carry the equipment by yourself. Committees can be tiresome, unwieldy groups of people who may have come out for the evening just to enjoy a social and a chit-chat. However, if you have a committee that operates efficiently and decisively it can relieve you of much of the time-consuming but necessary work and allow you to get to grips with the real nitty-gritty and keep a good overview without getting bogged down by details.

Obviously you do not need a full scale committee if you are planning a Bring and Buy sale in your garden. But when you are dealing with money from the public or money intended for donation it is always worth having at least a cashier or a treasurer as a second person to check your float, balance or banking. You never want to be put in the position of having the finger of doubt or suspicion pointed at you even if you know that you are entirely innocent. If you are working within an already established organisation such as the WI or a Hobbies Club you will be able to draw on an established committee structure.

For larger programmes or neighbourhood events involving several strata of the community, it is probably to your advantage to form a committee and possibly even agree on a constitution, especially if the event is to become an annual tradition.

COMMITTEES

So, now you are planning to work with a committee. It must run efficiently and professionally and have members who are whole-heartedly committed to the event.

Many committees that I have worked with have been largely comprised of business people, school teachers, local politicians, artists or people with a burning interest in the main theme of the event, in other words, people from all walks of life and profession but each with a separate skill or interest in a unique area.

Often I have been the 'enabler' without being a committee member. I found this worked well for me as I felt the members looked to me for unbiased advice, sometimes I acted as a catalyst in bringing about difficult decisions without having my own ideas to push forward. In this way you can truthfully say that any unpopular decision was brought by the committee and is not your responsibility alone; slightly a case of passing the buck, I know, but it makes for a quieter life and it will be you at the sharp end.

However, for those who want to be a leading light within a committee or those who are experts in their own fields, you will want to be very much part of the decision making team.

COMMITTEE MEMBERS

In every committee you will need a Chairman or Chairwoman, Secretary, Treasurer and then the people with special responsibilities which will change for every event. These can often include; advertising and marketing, sponsorship and prizes, programmes, volunteers, equipment, music and bands, catering, box office etc. Sometimes this is called an executive committee if your membership is very large and these people will be present at every meeting and make fundamental decisions. You may also need professional help in the way of specially invited members who may or may not be co-opted onto the non-executive committee. These could be a Police representative, a local politician, council officer, member of the Chamber of Commerce etc.

The Chair is usually the person who pulls every thing together, but s/he does not have to be. S/he does have to be able to direct a meeting authoritively and be able to cut through the discussion and arguments to the nub of the problem. It helps if s/he is used to this type of work, but it is not mandatory as long as s/he is clear thinking and assertive.

Similarly it is to your advantage to have people suited to other executive positions in the committee. An accountant makes an obvious choice for Treasurer and someone used to taking minutes and with access to a typewriter for Secretary.

Take a democratic decision on who will take the post of chief organiser (I assume that you are reading this book because it falls to you!). And make sure that you get copies of everything - even notes of telephone conversations. If other people are in charge of difficult sections, you must have an overview of the whole for it not to become chaotic and you may need to take over in an emergency.

KEY POINTS

❶ Decide if your event warrants a full committee or if you can manage with two or three central organisers.

❷ Chose a core committee and vote for a chairman/woman.

❸ Decide if you need more people to make up a non-executive committee but try to keep your group compact.

❹ Agree on dates for meetings and their regularity.

❺ Discuss the need for a constitution.

Good communications are vital for the smooth running of any event but equally you need to make it clear that you are only keeping a watching brief over other people's patches and that you will only interfere if invited or if the rest of the event may be jeopardised.

PRESIDENTS AND SPECIAL MEMBERS

Sometimes it is thought to be beneficial to appoint a President and even a series of Vice Presidents. The President usually takes the form of a 'figurehead' post, a V.I.P. to add weight to the credibility and a name to put prominently on stationery and advertisements.

Many events, especially those on the larger end of the scale are sponsored by one organisation or company. It is politic to invite a representative (if they haven't already insisted on one) to be on the committee or at least act as an observer to ensure that their generous donation is being spent as they would wish. They may only wish to have the minutes of each meeting sent to a named member of the company. If they are not interested in being an active part of the team they might welcome an invitation for a senior member of the company to be a Vice President.

Volunteers are ideal for stewarding or ushering roles. Lions Clubs, Scout Groups, Round Table, Rotarians or even a youth Sports Club are all ripe for persuasion as long as they are able to wear their own uniforms or strip and have a donation from the proceeds for their own cause. Again a member from the chosen group will need to have a place on the committee.

MEETINGS

Now. How often do all these people have to meet up? And how will we find a date to suit all of them every time? In my experience meetings need not be held more frequently than once a month and this gives you the obvious chance to select say, every last Tuesday or 21st of each month. This way members can mark their diaries well in advance and try to avoid other engagements. This is pretty elementary stuff, I know, but I am amazed at the number of committees who arrange the next meeting at the one just prior. The exception is the final meeting just before the Big Day. No more than a week before you need an opportunity to run through everyone's duties on site, hand out radios (and chargers) if used and iron out any last minute problems that may present themselves. Make sure that everyone is aware of alternative arrangements if circumstances change.

Meetings do not have to be long and if the committee is running a show that has an annual tradition then frequently decisions will go through on the nod, the members know just what is expected of them and the meeting serves as an 'aide memoire'.

Do be prepared, though, to sit through a lot of discussion and hear many different points if it is a new event. The democratic method is seldom swift and is as good a reason as any for keeping your committee as compact as possible.

This is a medium scale event and Bill has seven main committee members, of which he himself is one, and five observers. Twelve people in all, not all of whom will come to the meetings and not a bad sized committee.

Bill's position is as co-ordinator, general letter writer, planner (although that is open to discussion) and hirer of extras like caterers, ring entertainment, dog-professionals and organising all the other necessities such as site plotting, schedules, facilities and utilities, infrastructure, security, first-aid, sound system, and community relations.

His biggest problem will be confining decisions to the meetings. He is fond of his sister Molly and sees her and his friend Arthur two or three times a week. It is easy to chat about the event but he must remember to keep his committee in the picture and not go ahead with activities that have not been properly discussed.

CONSTITUTIONS

Do you need a constitution? Does Bill need a constitution? To answer the second question first, Bill probably does not need a constitution for this show. If it was to become an annual event, grow larger and perhaps have the parade through the town's main shopping street then his committee might benefit from a more formal arrangement.

A constitution does not have to be a complicated document; it may be that you should not be able to make decisions at any meeting at which there are less than three members or that you need your aims and objectives clearly spelled out so that they are not lost sight of over the years. Your constitution makes these legal requirements and can consist of one side of A4. In general the simpler you make it the better. If you are interested in writing a constitution there are publications which can assist you in more detail listed at the back of this book.

▶▶ BILL'S PROGRESS

Let's see what Bill Pincher is up to. Just to refresh your memory; he wants a dog-awareness exhibition, some trade stands, a pre-show parade, a dog show, some entertainers for the show ring, programmes to sell, a Police dog demonstration and some space for professionals to be involved. He has decided that he does not have the time or expertise to organise the show himself so has formed the core of his committee. He could do this before he chose a date and venue but he has already sorted out his venue with his friend Arthur. Together they went to see the local school headmaster who suggested that they choose the last week of the Summer term so that he would have maximum time to help organise the parade, but could guarantee that all the children would still be about.

After a few informal preliminary talks in the 'Bowl and Whistle' they form their committee.

Chairman - Bill could have put himself up for this post but he felt that he did not have the experience so he has asked a local businessman known to have community interests to join the committee, and he was voted Chairman.

Treasurer - Trainee accountant who lives on the estate. He went to the local school and his sister is still there.

Secretary - Chairman's own secretary who is prepared to help out for a small honorarium Dog Show

Dog Show Secretary - Rufus Byte, owner of Calamity Kennels

Trade Stands - Arthur Pint as he has good contacts with most of the local trades and crafts people in the area

Parade - Teacher from the local Middle School.

Organiser - Bill himself. He plans to take on all other activities.

There are other invited members who you will hear more about in other chapters. They receive minutes and occasionally come to meetings and include:

- Parks Officer from Local Council from whom they are hiring the Community Centre and Recreation Area.

- Representative of local Slurp 'n Yum Dog Biscuit Company who are donating the prizes and providing sponsorship.

- RSPCA representative. This could be Bill, but the RSPCA might want a more objective view.

- Police representative for the community relations side and the demonstration. After clearing it with his superior, Bill's friend the dog-handler will be the rep.

- Features writer for local paper which is supplying a free broadsheet as a programme paid for by advertising.

5 CONTACTING THE PROFESSIONALS

The ultimate professional to contact is someone to organise your show for you, but in this instance I assume that you are reading this guide because you are wanting to do it yourself. To employ a co-ordinator is expensive and really should be left to those whose events are being televised, or are very specialised such as sports meetings, or perhaps those very large-scale events being run as a business for personal gain. However there are others who can help or at least give free advice.

CUTTING RED TAPE - OR HOW TO TALK TO YOUR LOCAL AUTHORITY

It is always a good idea to inform your Local Authority of your events, however small they are, and even if you are to use a private building or land. You can get access to listings and entries into tourist guides and you may well find that they are eligible for a small community grant if you fulfil the Council's criteria (see Chapter 14). Your Local Authority may also have mobile loos, fencing, marquees, bunting, ticket booths, in fact all sorts of equipment available for hire or even for free. Don't forget the Parks and Gardens department might be able to supply display plants for VIP and tea tents. Actually I say 'free', but as you no doubt have been told before, 'There is no such thing as a free lunch'. However you might find that the services demanded in return aren't too onerous: a mention on the publicity here, a word in the programme there or a space to put an information stand.

The most useful person to contact, if you are doing anything other than the strictly keep-it-in-the-back-garden type of event, is the Council Promotions Officer (given a variety of titles from Events Promoter, Leisure Officer, Recreation Manager, Community Affairs officer etc.). To find the right person, ring the central Administration Office of your Local Council, i.e. where the Poll Tax / Council Tax demands come from. The number will be clearly marked in the telephone directories. This is usually the City or Town Hall or District Offices. Ask for the Public Events organiser and if asked 'which department?' suggest Leisure or Recreation or

Amenities. They will find the right person from that description.

Once again, I apologise if I appear to be starting at absolute basics here, but Local Authorities or Government Departments can be the stuff of nightmares if you don't know exactly what you want. When I worked for Stevenage Borough Council the telephonists changed so often that they didn't know who I was and when the caller was finally put through to me s/he was frequently so frustrated that it took a while to get the conversation calm enough to proceed. You can skip all this if you know the systems - but if not...well it just might save you a corker of a headache and save some Council Officer from getting their ear bent!

Having got hold of the right Officer, suggest a meeting and allow an hour to visit the Department to explain what it is that you want to do, let the Officer make suggestions and advise how they can assist. It helps not to go armed with a list of demands because, with hundreds of organisations all wanting help, it is tempting for them to pick and choose the easy options. By all means enquire about grants, but be prepared to have to put your entire event from objectives to budget on paper and then submit it to a selection committee and all for just a few hundred pounds. It is sometimes worth it as it can make all the difference in balancing the books, but it is extra work. (More about this in Chapter 14).

KEY POINTS

1 Develop a good contact at your Local Authority well in advance and keep the information flowing.

2 Explore ready made channels for obtaining equipment and funds.

3 If you think you may need to hire Council owned property - book it up to a year in advance, especially for popular dates such as Bank Holidays. You can always cancel if reasonable notice is given.

4 Check and double check your contract.

5 Tell the truth the whole truth and nothing but the truth to the Police; they are frequently extremely helpful and will be your best friends in a crisis.

6 Events involving road closure must be considered many months in advance and planned in great detail.

7 Let specialist institutions and clubs do some of the hard graft and don't forget that they have often done all this before and can provide useful advice.

8 Give the traditional 'tea and buns' groups a chance, rather than always going for specialist caterers.

9 Consider professional acts for part of your show. They add some glamour and give you something special for the billing. But read the contracts carefully as above.

10 Remember, red tape is there to be cut and it is easy if you know the person with the scissors!

21

If you plan to use Council land then this must be booked in advance, even up to a year in advance for popular days, and all sorts of constraints may be placed on you. Bylaws may exist to keep open footpaths or there may be limitations imposed on selling food, i.e. you may only be able to sell tea in plastic cups and wrapped foods such as sweets and biscuits. The hire fee may be waived for a charitable event, but you could just as easily find yourself paying up to £500 a day for a central site.

Read your contract carefully before you sign it. You may be planning a circus event but your Local Authority may have a policy of no performing animals; or a dinner dance to see the New Year in, and the venue's licence runs out at 11.30pm due to noise to surrounding buildings. Make sure it is the right venue for your event. (See Chapter 3 on choosing a venue). If you are happy with the contract keep a copy (or photocopy it) and return one, signed and dated. If you have a committee it might be an idea to let the other members take a look at it at the next meeting, someone else might see a problem that you have overlooked. Once the contract is signed there is no going back and usually there will be a fairly hefty deposit to put down also. And you must adhere to the rules. If you need to submit the names of traders 28 days in advance or produce a copy of your insurance certificate two months in advance, you really have to do it. Try not to let them have to chase you, however busy you are, it makes for a strained relationship and may jeopardise future plans. (If you know you have a problem with this read Chapter 11 on Time management and check lists). If you really can't do something by the time stated, let your contact know why and ask for an extended date.

The Officer may wish to be sent minutes or even sit on the committee, so it is a good idea to make the offer. When it comes near to the show, if you have been well looked after, send a letter to the Head of Department, thanking him/her for the Officer's time and enclosing a few free tickets or a car pass as a token of appreciation. This goes for all who help such as sponsors or donators of prizes etc. - you will find that this can help to oil the bureaucratic cogs and may work wonders when you want to repeat the event next year! However don't put council officers or other officials in the embarrassing situation of having to refuse a gift because it is too generous and might be construed as a bribe, however well-meant.

NATIONAL TRUST, HERITAGE LAND AND RESERVES

Not all land in Britain is private or Government owned, of course. Large areas of land that the public has access to is administered by charities and trusts. Permission is sometimes granted by the controlling bodies to hold events on this land but due deference must be given to their requests. Applications should be made well in advance to the local relevant organisation; they will, almost certainly, take it to their headquarters for a decision so don't expect to hear whether you have been successful for several weeks.

POLICE

It is a courtesy to inform the police of any event if you expect over 75 to 100 visitors and if there is any possibility of over a hundred or more people coming by car the Police will certainly need to know.

Find the local Police Station covering the area where the event is to be held by looking in the telephone directory as before. All Police forces insist that the first approach is made in writing to the Divisional Commander. He will pass the letter on to the appropriate officer who will reply and become your contact. Nine times out of ten, and always if there are traffic implications, s/he will want a brief meeting with you as an individual or ideally an invitation to attend a preliminary meeting with your committee. Remember, despite the impression that you very occasionally get from some individual Officers, you are only informing the Police to hopefully gain their cooperation and help; you do not actually have to ask their permission - excluding Public Order issues of course, but you would be well advised to go along with Police suggestions as they could seek an injunction to prevent the activity from taking place at all or stop it as soon as it has started on the grounds that you are causing an obstruction. If you intend having alcohol for sale or closing roads you will need permission and be required to give, at the very least, three months warning; for any other event four weeks will usually be enough.

If the access is restricted, be prepared for the Police to put 'no parking' cones along the road so that people cannot block the public highway. Make sure that you have enough spaces within the car park. (See Chapter 10 on dimensions for car parks). They will also wish to know if you intend selling liquor on a temporary licence, unless this will be from a bar of a building that is already licensed (see Chapter 16).

If you suspect that your event might attract an unruly audience that intend to make full use of the available alcohol or even bring their own, it may be advisable to air your fears with the Police in an informal way rather than try to deny the potential problem. Far better to arrange for areas to be contained or emergency procedures to be pre-planned than for it all to go horribly wrong and even for accidents or injuries to occur that might have been preventable. In my experience the Police are not going to be satisfied with belittling a problem and they will be less likely to assist or be lenient if they begin to suspect that the organiser is irresponsible. Show them that you are prepared to listen and take advice.

Even during a quiet, daytime activity the Police may need to be called. Accidents do happen, stock can escape or unleashed dogs cause havoc, fights break out or someone crashes a car. Ask your contact Officer for an emergency number and if possible the name of the Duty Officer for that day. Ensure that the number is given to your key personnel on the day and that you all know where the nearest telephone is. You will probably never need to use it, but better to be safe than sorry.

CLOSING ROADS

I love closing off roads! What a sense of power! But it can cause a great deal of frustration and upset to local residents and motorists if it is not approached with sensitivity.

Processions, carnivals or fiestas tend to take place in town or city centres and, by the nature of the beast, they are on the move. In some instances this means closing the highways to traffic. This sort of provision needs many months of preparation as Police, Local Authorities traffic planners and the residents or local shop owners along the roadside all need to consulted. Having agreed that the road could be closed in principle - and you will never get everyone to say 'yes'. A report has to be submitted for agreement in committee by local councillors, and procedures laid down. Due warning has to be published and the times of closure kept to a minimum. Occasionally a short, fairly fast moving procession can be integrated with the traffic thereby causing little disruption and this is clearly easier to arrange. A city centre event will attract a

> *I love closing off roads! What a sense of power!*

large crowd and is an exciting event to organise, it is also one of the few times that you can take your event to the audience rather than wait for them to come to you. You will, however, need a good many reliable stewards and helpers and you have to work closely with the Police at all times - they really have to co-ordinate this bit for you.

A few years ago all Police services came free. Now, most forces make a charge for extra duties; usually per constable per hour. In Norwich during 1992 this fee was £57 for the first two hours (minimum) and £28.50 for each subsequent hour. At 150 constables and specials for a large-scale street procession running over several hours you are looking at big money. However, I am told that the price can be negotiable, especially for charity events. It is always worth asking.

Things can still go wrong despite your best efforts. I once arranged for a vintage car rally to roll slowly through Norwich city centre to end up in the central gardens as a static display. The only entrance suitable for vehicles was down a narrow road next to a factory.

Two days prior to the rally the planned route into the city was dug up by the gas board and blocked off. The hole was at least six feet deep and went right across the whole road. We thought we had solved all our problems by laying extremely heavy duty metal sheeting over it, but worse was to occur. On arriving at the gardens at 7.30 in the morning to prepare for the static display, I was horrified to find an immense crane parked beside the entrance to the park completely obstructing the entrance. It had come to aid some weekend maintenance on the factory, and was totally immovable as the driver had gone for his breakfast. In this case it was just possible for the cars to squeeze past half on and half off the pavement, but we had to remove a sizable chunk of fencing to allow them to swing into the gardens.

This just goes to prove that you have to think of all the improbable as well as all the probable problems or at least notify everyone you can think of weeks in advance.

FIRST AID ORGANISATIONS

The St. John Ambulance Brigade and the Red Cross are the two main bodies in Britain who are prepared to give their services free of charge to events all around the country. They need to be booked well in advance and for a small event just a couple of staff on foot may be all that is required. For a large event, they may suggest bringing a vehicle or a tent and you will need to plan a space in the centre of the site and telephone access may be necessary for real emergencies. If you are indoors then a specially designated room or portacabin close to the main building will have to be available. You will find the local headquarters listed in the Yellow Pages for your area. A donation is always welcomeas they are also working with volunteers as a charitable organisation.

ASSOCIATIONS AND INSTITUTIONS

If you are planning a specialist event, e.g. a MG car rally, a yoga demonstration, an exemption dog show, etc., you will no doubt know of the organisation for your special interest such as MG Owners Club, Iyenga Yoga Foundation, or the Kennel Club of Great Britain. They are well worth contacting as some are keen to help with events of this kind. They may be able to assist with funding or providing anything from Judges to rosettes or VIPs to publicity material, very often free of charge. At the very least you will get your event listed in a specialist magazine or handbook. Some events, such as pedigree animal shows or some sporting events must be registered or at least granted approval by the relevant parent organisations.

If you are not sure who to approach for help in a particular field, try going to your local newsagent and ask to see a list of titles of magazines for that subject, they may have what you want in stock and if not can certainly order you one to get ideas from. For even more unique subject matters, where magazines are available on subscription only such as 'Decanter', 'Carriage Driving', or 'Jalopy' etc. then the central library is your best bet, where you will find Benn's Press Directory and Willing's Press Guide in the reference section. Remember these very useful tomes when you come to advertise a specialist event.

And now to the Womens Institute. If you do not wish to be so grand or extravagant as to warrant a catering company, remember that the WI have been running tea tents and cake stalls for time immemorial. They may well jump at the chance to make a bit of money for the Institute. You will not gain any financial reward but you will get a friendly and often efficient service for little outlay and you will have one more facility to offer to your public. If the WI are booked up you can ask your local Guide or Scout Troop especially if the event is appealing to a younger end of the market.

ACTS AND AGENTS

The easiest way to fill your show if you need a few professional acts is to buy the current copy of the 'Showman's Directory'. This lists all sorts of entertainment and also any contractors or services and equipment that you might need, and is available mail-order from the address listed at the back of this book. 'Showcall' is another publication that you might find useful - it deals entirely with entertainers and again is available mail order. This two volumed directory is published annually and lists acts, entertainers and experts in one volume and agents and civic halls in the other. In short if you have money and copies of 'Showcall' and the 'Showman's Directory' you can put together a very promising show.

Another source of entertainers or expertise is the weekly theatrical newspaper, 'The Stage'. You can buy a copy of 'The Stage' off the shelf at any large newsagents or they should be able to order it for you.

One word of warning when booking professionals: read the contracts very carefully and particularly check whether you still have to pay if the artiste fails to arrive due to accident, bad weather, poor directions etc. Also check your insurance in case you have to cancel the show for any reason; you will probably still have to pay for the act if they have turned up in good faith.

6 PUBLICITY

There is an old saying 'You can't afford not to advertise', and nowhere is that statement more true than in planning one-off events. Today's public are sophisticated, critical and independent. They make up their own minds about what to do for the day. No longer do they have to wait for the works outing or the annual visit from the circus. 55% of families own a car, over 35% take a foreign holiday once a year, virtually everyone can read or at least has someone in their family who can and now with over 90% of households having access to a television they can have entertainment without even leaving their armchairs every single minute of the day.

There is, however, something unique and special about going out for your leisure, especially to an outdoor show. You cannot share the television with hundreds of other people. You cannot record the atmosphere and you cannot yet recreate the special noise and smells that are associated with an exciting, raucous, slightly frightening visit to the fair on a warm summer evening. Even something as proper and English as a Tea Dance held on a weekday afternoon in the local Village Hall has a kind of companionship and shared enjoyment that cannot be found elsewhere.

These moods are peculiar to the individual event and it is the anticipation of experiencing heightened emotions that is going to attract your customers. Of course they may want to actually have the opportunity to buy a 1959 Corgi model of a Ford Zephyr estate, but if that was all, they would buy it mail order through a catalogue. There is the occasional member of the audience who just has to hear Ave Maria one more time, but again if that was all there was to it she would take out her Jessye Norman CD and play it again. No, what you are offering is live, shared entertainment and usually, just that one opportunity.

Enough of my homespun psychology. But it serves to remind you that there is more to selling events than just the booked entertainment.

In the following sections of this chapter you will find some basic marketing ideas for your event. It is a lengthy subject and one that is really too involved to do full justice to within this guide. Marketing should be absolutely unique to each and every event and a separate marketing plan should be drawn up for each one.

Some good books for further reading on the subject are listed at the back of this book.

MARKETING

All the methods you can think of that are going to generate an audience for your event can come under the blanket title of Marketing. These include studying your market, pricing, public relations, merchandising, sales and promotions, media, printing and design, tasters, signage and probably more that I have yet to come across.

I shall tackle advertising, printing and design, tasters (pre-event events) and local signage separately and in greater detail later in the chapter.

Before putting on any event you have to study your market. It is impossible to satisfy all of the people all of the time but you have to identify your attenders, and if you aim to widen the audience you need to know who might come if the price was right, if a coach park was available or whatever. It is also

KEY POINTS

1. You cannot afford to give marketing a miss.
2. Identify your attenders and the intenders.
3. Bring the flavour of your event into your publicity.
4. Consider all aspects of marketing as outlined above.
5. Make a marketing plan that is unique to every event.
6. Target your publicity.
7. Remember there are more ways of making money than relying on an entrance fee.
8. Ensure that your event suits your sponsors, landlord and cause.
9. Always use the golden rules for advertising.
10. Negotiate prices for everything.
11. For larger events use the professionals to take the chore out of signing.
12. Consider pre-event activities and launches.
13. Work to a timescale and stick to it. Allow more time than you think is strictly necessary.

important to know who definitely will not come even if you gave them free tickets and arranged for a mini-bus to come and pick them up. You don't want to waste money and effort in including them in your advertising plans.

Only you will know who your potential market is and where you can find them; and if you don't, then you should have conducted some basic market research before you even decided on an event to ascertain that you at least had a market out there. One way to start is to think of your potential audience in groups (socio-economic, geographic, religious, age, family status etc.) and in particular which newspapers and magazines they would read; this gives you a pretty good idea where to place your press ads for a start. Then look at the ads they are already running, especially the classified section, and this can direct you to special interest clubs or weekly meetings to which you can advertise direct.

Keep a picture of the typical punter in your mind all through your marketing campaign and if you don't waiver from your original decision you won't go far wrong.

PRICING AND PROMOTIONS

Pricing is possibly the most important and the most difficult aspect of marketing. If you don't get this right then one of two things can happen. You get plenty of people to the show but you don't make any money or you get very few because they can't afford the tickets. Either way you can end up with egg on your face and the problem of not knowing how your expenses will be covered.

You can only tell if you have got the price right if you do your budgeting properly (see chapter 12). Very simply, add all your estimated expenditure together, don't forget anything, work out how many tickets you are likely to sell - go to other similar events to get an idea of this and look at other pricing policies - multiply numbers by ticket price, remember to include concessions and check the profit margin. Prices might vary around the UK or between town and country so cut your cloth accordingly. There is no point charging what you think the show was worth in the Home Counties at £4.00 a ticket, if you know that the local public in Merseyside is only used to spending £2.50. The only exception to the rule is where you hold an annual event that is a 'Spectacular'. The public get to know that each year is bigger and better, they have had value for money on the last occasion and look forward to another visit on the same day the next year. At this stage you can begin to charge at a different rate to your competitors. But the golden rule is to charge as much as you can get. Which doesn't mean, charge as much as you like. As Keith Diggle points out in his 'Guide to Arts Marketing', 'If we charge more than people will pay, then we get nothing'.

Many Local Authorities, especially Labour controlled Councils, will only allow you to hire their property if you agree to considerable concessionary reductions for members of the community on Income Support, Old Age Pensions and so on - yet another reason to read your contract carefully. Of course as well as being morally ethical this can work to your long term advantage. If you can attract a wider audience, including people who would not traditionally be interested in your specialist event, through wise concessionary pricing bands you may make some converts and increase your potential audience for future events. (More about selling tickets and other ways of raising income in Chapter 13). In a few limited situations it may be possible to offer sales or discounts on tickets and entry fees for more than one event.

▶▶ BILL'S PROGRESS

Bill has discovered that there will be four separate dog shows held in his area between May and September. He meets with the three other organisers and works out that they can save money if they share a publicity leaflet with an application form attached for the appropriate schedule. These are aimed at the dog owners keen on showing their animals, not at the general public: the event posters will be kept separate and aimed at the visiting audience as each show has a different flavour and, of course, Bill wants to highlight his RSPCA connections. Each leaflet advertises all four shows and any owner wanting to show his dogs in all four shows gets one show free i.e. they only pay 75% of the full price. The organisers divide the discounted fee between everyone.

After the leaflet is published, Bill finds himself summoned to his Senior Officer's office. He is praised for his activities and his commitment to educating the public. But he is also severely hauled over the coals for not clearing his agreement to team up with the other dog shows for the schedules. The RSPCA are not happy being associated with one dog show in particular as it has acquired a poor reputation in the past.

Bill's idea can work in other ways. One suggestion is to promote a minority interest event through another popular event by offering discounts, for example tickets for two popular events purchased together give you a half-price ticket for the less popular show. Other incentives might include a free drink in the interval, '£1.00 off' leaflets or even discounts for large parties. The permutations are endless and you only have to walk round your local supermarket to see ideas that can be adapted.

Many sites are too large and impractical to fence off so you cannot sell entrance tickets. Mobile events such as parades are obviously impossible to ticket because of the transient nature of the crowd and, you hope, the high numbers, so you need to be sure of making your money elsewhere such as sponsorship, selling trade stand plots, raffles, programmes etc. You will find other methods of raising money in Chapter 13.

Is all this marketing? Well perhaps not, in the strict sense of the word but you will still have to price your programmes or raffle tickets or even plots correctly to encourage people to buy.

PUBLIC RELATIONS AND THE MEDIA

For a one-off event you may not be able to get involved in serious public relations. But the way you and your committee conduct yourselves and handle the event will all add to public perception, both of your ability as organisers and of the cause for which you are raising money if that is one of your aims. If you are planning to work again as an operational group and/or to hold the event as an annual occasion then that all-important first impression has to be a good one. You need your colleagues and the public to trust and believe in you.

If you are planning a Green Festival that is to highlight conservation, vegetarianism and environmental awareness for instance, you would raise your credibility if your stationery, posters and tickets were all printed on recycled materials. Your 'street-cred' would be severely damaged if you then allowed a hog-roast to take one of the trade stands. This illustrates the need to plan everything even down to the last vegi-burger; and for the chief organiser to have a complete overview.

For some events you need to take a serious political look at the whole. You may see a gap in the market for a Wizards and Warlocks' Parade but you need to know that you will offend some people if you start it off from the Cemetery attached to local Church. Equally you might well be asking for trouble if you invited a prominent figure from CND to open the fete held on a meadow belonging to Col. Blimp (rtd). without clearing it with him first.

The media can play a big part in your event if you let them and local radio is one of the most helpful mediums especially if you have made friends with one individual presenter.

Start by sending, about a month in advance, a package containing a press release, some hand bills and an invitation with a covering letter explaining any local angle or connection that they may be interested in; this could be a popular VIP, fundraising for a local project or just trying something unique to the area. Always include two contact names with their daytime telephone numbers in your letter and suggest that you will make a follow up call in a week's time. More often than not you will get a call asking you to explain your event a little more. Sometimes you might get an invitation to appear on one of the shows to talk about one aspect of your event. These are usually done live with a little practice before as to what questions you will be asked. Come to the interview well prepared with some notes for yourself if necessary and some more handbills, and your own name and position on a piece of paper for the presenter to have in front of him/her.

If you think your show might have local television impact then you can follow the same procedure as above for the regional TV station in your area. They will be less likely to contact you and you might well have to make a follow up call. Even if you get as far as being interviewed there is no guarantee that it will be broadcast. Television is very immediate and your event will not be able to compete with the Town hall catching fire at three in the afternoon. But given that summertime is the 'silly season' in journalism, you just might get lucky.

Newspaper and magazine articles are often read by hundreds of people, so cultivate a features writer and keep the link fresh by sending in press releases and photographs to keep the interest going. Suggest running competitions with the paper or allow them to compile an advertising feature on the back of a free programme. You will have to let them have a list of trade stands and sponsors for them to sell advertising space to make it pay. You may even find that for 'in association with...' on all your publicity that you can negotiate free press ads. This is well worth the effort!

ADVERTISING

Advertising is communicating. You can make people hear about your event if you hire the town crier and he 'Oyezes' your event from the street corners; but the shoppers might be too busy debating the price of sweetcorn in the local market and not want to listen; so you have not communicated. You need to place your publicity where it will be seen or heard otherwise it will be a complete waste of time and money. Having got people to notice it and so attracted their attention, you need to make sure you are telling them everything they need to know.

The golden rules for any event advertisement are:
1. What is it?
2. Where is it?
3. When is it?

From these three things your potential audience knows what to expect, where to find it and at what date and time to be there.

For perfect publicity you can also add the following elements:
1. The name of the organisers and a contact name and telephone number
2. What is it for? If you happen to be fundraising
3. How much does it cost to get in?

Where do you advertise? Absolutely anywhere that your potential audience might be. It is helpful to think of getting value for money with each handbill and poster. If you hand deliver leaflets through letterboxes they have to be the right letterboxes as they will have a limited readership. However if you put a poster up in the local community centre or village hall you will get many different people all looking at your one poster.

Other places to think about for posters and handbills are: inserts in the local free paper (potentially expensive, but might be worth it - a press ad. may be better value), the central library - libraries often do a distribution service around their branches, health centres, pubs and restaurants, council poster sites outside car parks or by bus stops and taxi lines, public lifts, hospitals, company canteens, garages, local shops, the event's venue itself, parks notice boards - with permission, council offices - especially rates halls, Tourist Information Centres, bus and train stations, other tourist attractions or even other events.

Of course you need not restrict yourself to posters and hand-bills. (Look at the section above, under 'Public Relations and the Media', on how to negotiate press publicity). For an arts event, why not think about printing card bookmarks with your publicity and giving them away with each book borrowed at the library or sold at a sympathetic bookshop? What about beer mats in the pub for a Beer Festival? Or table napkins in local restaurants for a Medieval Banquet? On a date that the restaurant is closed, of course! Get permission from the Council to fly a flag, hang a banner over the road or paint footprints on the pavement using washable paints showing the way to your show.

PRINT AND DESIGN

How you choose to design and print your publicity material can help to form those all-important first impressions.

Designers seem expensive but they needn't be; most enjoy working on publicity material, it is quick and they can let their imagination loose. They also know how to keep to a budget if presented with a maximum figure for the likely print costs as well as the design fee. So although it is tempting to get Harry - who is pretty mean with a paintbrush - on the job, it may not be your best option. One source of exciting design talent that I have used in the past is the local Art and Design College. They may even have a print shop in which to make the finished posters but they will need notice to fit it into the term's work.

Printers are very competitive and you would do well to ask for quotations from several companies. If you like what one printer produces, but prefer another's price, then negotiate until you get what you want. Remember to ask important questions such as how long they need from receiving the art work, whether they can prepare the art-work 'in-house' from a layout or whether you can have a discount if you collect direct.

Make sure that you understand the prices of coloured paper or extra ink colours. Sometimes if you give good advance notice you might be able to have an extra colour printed back to back with another job in the same ink. The extra cost is not so much the cost of the fancy inks but the cost of washing down the machine and wasting time and paper getting the new colour properly distributed.

PRE-EVENT EVENTS

Some events are just crying out to be given a taster session. By this I mean taking an active role in advertising, by taking a little hint of what is to come to your potential audience rather than wait for them to read the publicity flyers and decide to come to you. It can be as low key as sending a couple of jugglers to the town square before a circus skills workshop or taking half the cast of the panto to the local department store to act out some of the scenes before a signing session.

At Stevenage I once planned to drive a horse drawn hearse, complete with black plumed horses and draped coffin on the back, all around the town with no other explanation than for a 'mourner' telling people to be ready - ready for what...? - at the Gordon Craig Theatre that night at 7.45pm. Sadly I couldn't find anyone near enough to supply the hearse but the three lugubrious characters dressed in top hats and tails that we used instead behaved in a very sinister fashion and managed to drum up a good late audience to our spoof Frankenstein show. Use your imagination and be as zany as you can. Tasters are a very immediate form of marketing. You can even have a temporary, mobile box-office selling tickets in a caravan near by.

LOCAL SIGNAGE

It does not matter how well you think your venue is known, there are bound to be people who have not heard of it so signs are always useful.

For a large event it may pay to ask the RAC or the AA to do road signs for you. I personally have no experience of the AA as I have always used the RAC, but both companies are very experienced in this work and can even cover the whole country. They offer very much the same service but it might be worth asking for a quotation from each as costs may vary from area to area. Addresses and telephone numbers can be found at the back of the book.

The RAC runs their signing service as a commercial operation from their headquarters in North London and your initial contact should be made six weeks in advance via their freephone number from anywhere in the UK. Assuming that they have not signed this particular event before they will need to know your name, address and telephone number, what date the event is to be held and where and what entrances you will be using. They will also like the suggested wording for the notices, an estimation of the size of the crowd and how many signs you think you will need. The signs officer can give you advice and work with you to obtain the answers so you do not need to be a traffic or signing expert. In 1992 the price for signing a new event was £150 plus VAT, this included the sign schedule, obtaining planning permission from the Local Authority and 10 signs put in place, usually 48 hours in advance. A further £15 each was payable for any extra signs. Like everything in the event world you may be able to negotiate a better rate so don't forget to ask.

For most events you will not need to go to the above lengths, but for any show, signs on the roadside i.e. on a Council owned verge, will probably need planning permission as they could cause a distraction to motorists. Signs on trees or posts overlooking the road but situated in private property such as fields or gardens are exempt. Don't attempt to put too much on a notice, the name of the event and an arrow may be all that is needed. One final point about road signs; think hard whether you need to include the date. If they are dated and you wish to repeat the event another year they will all have to be repainted. The day of the week may be all that is necessary.

Signs within the site are a different matter and are entirely up to you. The sort of signs that are useful are to direct the way to Car Parks, Loos, Refreshments, First Aid post, Lost Children reconciliation point, Secretary's tent or creche. Other events might need signs to grouped trade stands such as crafts, clothing, toys etc.

The best signs are painted on wood or metal and mounted on wooden stakes, hammered securely into the ground. However as long as they are weatherproof and reasonably firm any materials will do. Some estate agents use a kind of corrugated plastic for their 'For Sale' signs and this makes an excellent substitute if you can get hold of it. If your event is to become an annual tradition then it could be worth getting the signs screenprinted with a more permanent design for use another year.

7 INFRASTRUCTURE

Where does all that equipment that you see in use at events and shows come from? And how does it get there?

Even for a small 'do' in the Village Hall or a bring-and- buy sale in the back garden you need a certain amount of equipment. For very small scale events you may be able to supply all that you need from your own and your friends' houses, and the tables and chairs that you have borrowed are probably small enough to go into the back of a large estate car.

INDOOR EVENTS

If your show is to be in a public building such as a community centre, church or sports hall, most of what you will need is very likely to be available on site with or without an extra charge. You can expect chairs, tables, benches, podiums, stage risers and lecterns all to be fairly common requests. If an official 'cash desk' does not exist, then a very effective filter system can be made between a salesperson sitting at a table and another opposite on foot just to control the line. Basic stage lighting and public address systems are often 'in situ' but a full stage lighting rig might pose more of a problem. Most suppliers are listed in the Yellow Pages under Theatrical services or supplies. They should also be able to provide a sound system if necessary.

BARNS

For a Harvest Festival Party in a barn you will have to provide everything. Before you decide on holding an event in a barn, think of the possible fire hazard. They are really only safe as a venue if brick built and scrupulously swept clean of all combustible materials, such as straw and hay, and cleared of all chemicals and farm equipment.

Personally, parties in barns terrify me. I would rather hold an event in a marquee in a field than in a barn with possibly only one access and next to other buildings full of potential fire hazards. You have the added danger of alcohol consumption and smoking on the premises. If a barn is really your only option, then provide decent seating facilities. Never, never use bales of straw. Not only are they incredibly dangerous due to the fire hazards involved, but it could invalidate your insurance policy. Make sure that numerous buckets of sand are available for stubbing out cigarettes and provide fire extinguishers, suitably signed.

TABLES AND CHAIRS

For all events, if you cannot provide enough tables, trestles and chairs through your own contacts then possible sources might be: schools, village or church halls, leisure centres, or marquee firms. Some areas might have companies, again listed in Yellow Pages, who specialise in hire services for functions. Some education authorities sell off old school chairs at regular sales and this can be a good source of chairs, tables and desks if you think you are going to have a regular use for them.

OUTDOOR EVENTS

Events outside tend to pose more of a challenge. You have to build your own walls, doors and floors, as it were, before you start. Your walls will include: fencing - if it is used, parade rings, crowd control barriers, the shape and placing of stands and marquees and bumbling pins and ropes. (Bumbling pins are thin metal stakes with the tops curled over twice to hold a length of rope.) The box office, entrance gate or ticket booth are your doors and the floor is usually grass. Grass is, of course living vegetation and subject to the vagaries of the weather. Whilst it might have looked ideal when you chose the site in April, by July it could be a wilderness. Remember that it may need to be cut or

KEY POINTS

1. Try to think of all the equipment and facilities that you might need well in advance.

2. Remember to arrange for transport if extra items are not delivered.

3. Think hard before you decide to use a barn. They can be very dangerous.

4. You may be able to hire or borrow much of the equipment from your local council but you will find commercial suppliers listed in the telephone directories. Tool hire companies can be a good source.

5. Remember that grass might need cutting.

6. Ensure that you understand the needs and dangers of any generator that you might hire. Have a qualified electrician check all connections and lighting rigs before you open. Store the fuel in a safe place.

7. Check Chapter 16 for the Health and Safety at Work Act and read the relevant publications

8. A stand pipe may be vital if you involve animals, failing that you must be able to supply clean water using other means.

9. Make sure that all caterers are warned if water is not available on site.

protected with matting if the weather has been wet. Slippery grass is also dangerous and needs to be covered to prevent accidents. Matting is available from tent hire companies.

FENCING

The type of fencing that you use is dictated by the job you want it to do. If all you need is a demarcation line marking the boundaries of, perhaps, a car park then stakes and a rope will be quite adequate. However, if you are selling entry tickets you will need to be able to keep out those people who are bent on getting in for free. Here 5' chestnut paling at the very least will be necessary, especially if you have limited alternative security. This may be available from the Estates department or Direct Labour Organisation of your local council or possibly on hire from builders' suppliers, building or highway contractors or - at a greater cost - from Fencing Services companies, again in the Yellow pages. If you intend to erect the chestnut paling yourselves, you need as many volunteers as you can muster, some large sledge hammers and at least a day to do it in. It is very hard work and best left to contractors.

The safest fencing for parade rings, if you are showing horses or stock is to use good quality, interlocking crowd control barriers. They have the added advantage of operating very satisfactorily as gates which enables the whole ring to be sealed quickly if an animal escapes. I have known this to happen more than once at a Heavy Horse Show during the Young Handlers and Foal classes. A shire yearling, loose and going at full throttle is pretty unnerving and it definitely helps if you can keep it contained!

Crowd control barriers can be hired from your local council or failing that from national suppliers including SGB Readyfence and GKN Quickform who are based in Birmingham (addresses in the back of the book). There are other companies around the country supplying this sort of equipment. I have always used GKN and never had any problems. If you telephone 021-706 3399 they will put you in touch with your local depot. They need a week's notice, and preferably more as everything comes from a central store. Confirmation of the hire needs to be in writing, don't forget to include the site address for delivery or you just might end up with 300 barriers in your front garden! And, if you aren't a known organisation, they will require a cheque in advance with time to clear it. Be warned that the barriers and their feet will be delivered dismantled, and you will be required to put them together, which all takes more time on the day. For high security sites you can use a two metre high fencing called K/Fence, also supplied by the same company.

TENTS AND MARQUEES

Again you may be able to borrow tents from the Local Authority but there are any amount of hire companies available. Traditional canvas marquees with a ridge pole and guy ropes look the most attractive but take up more space than the more modern plastic coated, free-standing, rigid frame tents.

A more interesting way of tackling the weather problem is to use temporary inflatable buildings or a spectacular new canopy tent now available called variously a Sheltent or Pagoda that has the appearance of bird's wings. This has the added advantage of looking very welcoming as the opening structure is wide and airy.

For very small spaces or stands you could use a unique telescopic Mini Marquee that you can put up in a couple of minutes.

BOX OFFICES AND TICKET BOOTHS

The simplest form of ticket booths are made from folding 3" x 3" frames covered by plywood sheets or canvas to protect a free standing table and chair within. Most events can get away with no booths at all if they operate a good filter system made from crowd control barriers. Your decision as to which system to use may largely rest on what sort of event you are planning. Shows that are on the Arts end of the spectrum traditionally are entered through a box office. Fetes and fairs use crowd control barriers and sporting events may well use a turnstile system. It may just be down to aesthetics or finances in the end. Provided the cash is removed regularly to a secure store you should not have a problem, whatever you use. People, when looking forward to an event, are happy to stand in line as long as the queue can be seen to be progressing. If you know you will have a problem at peak periods, try keeping the crowd amused with buskers or at least display signs to indicate, say, '10 mins from here'. They can then make their own choice to stay or come back later. Another useful idea is to display a site plan next to the queue to tempt the public and help prevent the inevitable bunching that occurs just inside the gates whilst people decide what to see first.

UTILITIES

If you know that you are going to need electricity, gas or water on site then you need to check for availability. If you are using public property, a metered all weather electrical supply may well be connected and ready for use. It's not the end of the world if you get there and find that your perfect venue is without the facility you need as you can, if necessary, bring it with you.

Almost all tool hire companies will stock generators of varying sizes suitable for most electrical needs. As some are exceedingly heavy you may well have to arrange delivery, so make sure that it is left exactly where you planned, as you may not be able to move it yourselves. Small portable and semi-portable generators will probably run on petrol, the larger and more powerful ones will need diesel. Check with your supplier that you have enough fuel on site for all your needs and store it safely away from fire and out of the sun. Remember too that you will need an alternator (although this may be intergral) to convert your 'home-made' power into something that your equipment is more used to. Modern generators are much quieter than they used to be but you will still have to make sure that you have enough cable to place it far enough away to be sure of hearing an announcer or not to frighten animals.

For small and medium-scale events it is unlikely that you will need a three phase supply, however you may occasionally find that for certain types of usage it can work out cheaper than using single phase. If you use a generator capable of producing three phase electricity you will have the added advantage of having both three phase and single phase available if necessary. If a three phase supply is not on site you can again hire a generator or ask the local electricity board to connect a temporary supply. When using any electrical supply, and in particular three phase, it is prudent to have a qualified electrical engineer check all connections, leads and equipment. You have a responsibility to protect the public and you may be required to have the site checked by a qualified electrician by the terms of your contract or insurers.

Whilst virtually all buildings will be connected to mains electricity and water, not all will have mains gas supplies and, unless there is a cafe or clubhouse on a sports field or recreation ground, your outside venue will almost certainly be lacking a gas facility. Cooking, refrigeration and heating are the main needs for gas and all can be adequately provided for using propane. Suppliers of LPG (liquid petroleum gas) can be found in the

Yellow Pages under 'Bottled Gas'.

Water will be necessary if you are supplying refreshments or have animals as part of your show. Horses especially are very thirsty animals particularly in the Summer, and for a horse show you will need gallons of fresh water available. A stand pipe is ideal, but it is not always possible to provide or it may be just too far to carry buckets back and forth from one pipe on a very large site. Hosepipes are not adequate, they inevitably get trodden on or damaged and you will, consequently, lose your supply; and it has to be reliable. If a mains supply is impossible then you will have to have open tanks or clean drums regularly filled by a bowser. Most parks departments have access to bowsers or, if you are in the country, a friendly farmer may be able to come to your rescue.

Catering companies can be expected to make their own water arrangements but they need to be warned if none is available. If you are providing your own refreshments then ensure that you will be able to bring enough water with you.

▶▶ BILL'S PROGRESS

Gorridge Town Council have made the Community Centre and recreation ground available for £150. It should be more but they have lowered the fee as it is a charitable event.

The Dog Day is largely to be held outdoors, but the film show is planned for the Community Centre and the Girl Guides will be using the kitchen as a base for their catering operation. A metered electrical supply is also available from the Centre and will be used for the urns in the tea tent.

One spanner in the works manifested itself fairly early on. Bill had planned to seat everyone in the main hall of the Centre to watch the film, but the caretaker informed him that all the chairs were due to be re-covered in the Summer and would be unavailable on the date that Bill needed them.

After a week of sleepless nights, Bill raised the point at the next meeting. The chairman, John Wright - owner of the Red Tile Company - solved the problem by making an arrangement with his local parson. The Vicar agreed to lend 100 church hall chairs if John would supply one of his trucks and a driver to transport them.

8 VOLUNTEERS AND **DELEGATION**

When I first started in this business, my critics would say that one of my failings was an unwillingness to delegate. I hope that is no longer true, as in time I have come to realise the value of help, especially from the volunteer. Help can come in many forms apart from the obvious muscle and brawn. Support, encouragement and an infectious enthusiasm all come from working with people who have chosen to give their time and sometimes their belongings for a chosen cause.

There are many, many organisations who are prepared to put their members forward to help at events, particularly community and charity shows.

WHERE TO FIND HELP

Over the years, apart from numerous individuals who have all given their time freely, I have worked with Lions Clubs, Rotarians, Round Table, Scouts, Sea Scouts, Guides, schools and colleges, church groups, WI, Senior and Junior Chambers of Commerce, Venture Scouts, sports clubs, the Territorial Army, many companies' social clubs, Mother's Unions, hospitals, health groups, Trade Unions and university students.

Today you can cut your research time to minutes. With one telephone call to the Volunteer Centre UK (0442 873311) you can have access to the Volunteer Bureau Directory which tells you where the nearest Bureau is in your area. They will take details of your event and the sort of help that you are after and put you in touch with people who can help. Having said that, I have been told that some regions are not so fortunate as my own in providing an efficient Bureau so have some other sources up your sleeve, just in case.

All the local media are worth trying for assistance in finding volunteers. Some radio stations, in particular, actually run a regular programme or 'spot' for just this purpose. Regional TV companies may also broadcast social action programmes and your local newspaper might well be interested in running a feature or at the very least print a letter asking for help. There may also be a ready-made network of volunteers supporting the benefiting charity or other charitable organisations, such as Age Concern, may be happy to let you use their contacts.

WHAT YOU CAN EXPECT FROM VOLUNTEERS

There is one rule of thumb here. Let volunteers know exactly what job it is that they are volunteering for. They can then make the choice to put themselves forward or not. Hopefully there will be no misunderstandings and with any luck neither you nor your volunteers will get any nasty surprises. But don't expect anyone to do anything that you would not be prepared to tackle yourself!

In my experience, as long as they are prepared beforehand, people will have a go at almost anything. One wonderful 70+ member of the Lions helped me erect a scaffolding grandstand far into the night until it was complete. I have had teams of people putting up fencing for hours at a time in burning sunshine and taking it all down again in the pouring rain. One lively group of American Footballers regularly helped deliver and later collect crowd control barriers all around Norwich for the Lord Mayor's Street Procession and for another event members of a local Citizen's Band Radio Club were responsible for all the marshalling.

Of course, you have to be able to rely on your volunteers once they have offered their services. You need to make it clear that you expect a commitment from them and if they can't make it on a particular day or are going to be late, you need to know well in advance so that you can make alternative arrangements.

WHAT'S IN IT FOR THEM

Fun, companionship, satisfaction, a sense of responsibility or, conversely, allowing someone else to hold responsibility, an opportunity to get out of the house or a belief in the cause. But above all, we all need to feel needed and you will often find that the more you show that you need your volunteers the more they will be prepared to commit their time and energy to you, often time and time again. These are all reasons for people volunteering to help with events and if you, as leader, keep the atmosphere as light as possible by sharing the decisions and being flexible they will manage to get what they want out of the work and you will get a job well done.

TRAINING

It will be necessary to brief your volunteers carefully on their duties. Try to add a little of the background to the event and state your prime objectives but keep talks short and simple. It can help to give detailed instructions in written form as an addition to the verbal briefing session. Indeed if they are sent these in advance people will have a chance to ask questions if there is something that they are not quite happy with.

In some cases it might be important to arrange for some volunteers to undergo more formal training or at the very least a practice session. Those handling money might benefit from running through security procedures. Volunteers who are assisting at a dog show might want to spend a morning with the Local Authority Dog Warden or Police Dog Handlers to learn what to do in an emergency. Local Fire Brigades are also happy to train non-professionals in the use of fire-fighting equipment; especially useful for firework display stewards.

TO PAY OR NOT TO PAY?

I have always made it clear that I don't want anyone to be out of pocket. So, if someone has brought their pick-up truck to help haul equipment I have always offered the cost of the petrol or if lunch has been brought to the site for all the workers I have made sure that whoever was responsible was reimbursed.

The truth is that most volunteers do not expect even out-of-pocket expenses. However, if an individual or group of individuals are working from a club they may well be glad of a donation from the profits. If there are no profits, well...'c'est la vie'!

9 LOOS AND LITTER

This chapter concerns itself with what a crowd leaves behind after the show is over. The problem is almost entirely confined to outdoor events as any 'do' indoors is going to be in a building that has at least basic toilet facilities (except barns), and, perhaps with a few additions, enough ashtrays and waste bins to satisfy all needs.

GETTING RID OF THE RUBBISH

Let's look at litter first. It doesn't seem to matter how many bins you provide, the Great British public still prefers the ground. It does help, though, if you put the bins in the right places, i.e. right under their noses as they throw things away. Study the site to decide which places are likely to generate the most litter. These will include the entrance gate if you are selling tickets or programmes, all around refreshment tents, take away stands and ice cream vans, stalls where raffle tickets are used, bran tubs or lucky dips and cake stalls where a surprising amount of people are greedy enough to rip the wrappers off their chocolate crispy cakes and eat them there and then! Place your bins accordingly.

For small events a few ordinary domestic dustbins - minus the lids - lined with a black bag, and borrowed from friends will often be enough. A larger fete will need more bins and liners, which you may be able to borrow from the Environmental Health Department of your Local Authority, or at the very least, fence posts with a black bin liner securely fixed at one point so that it presents an open top. Where you are likely to have huge quantities of rubbish such as outside a multi-station burger bar you may have to go for large oil drums and ensure that they are emptied when full. In windy weather empty all bins when they are half full as rubbish soon starts to blow away if you allow it to accumulate.

For any but the smallest show, it is judicious to rent a skip of an appropriate size so that you do not have to cart car loads of garbage to the nearest tip. Even if the council has a collection service it will not be until after the weekend and food waste will attract dogs and vermin.

KEY POINTS

1. Allow enough bins and/or liners for the expected number of spectators.

2. Put bins in areas of most use.

3. Arrange for collection, a skip or to dump the rubbish yourselves.

4. Suit the type of sanitary provision to your budget and event, but make sure that whatever you choose is up to standard.

5. Check the terms of the Public Entertainment Licence if you have to have one (Chapter 16).

6. Ensure that the loos are cleaned and maintained throughout the day and arrange for them to be in a hygienic condition when you leave unless otherwise arranged.

7. Remember to provide facilities for disabled people and Mothers with babies if at all possible.

LOOS

Toilet facilities come in many different forms ranging from a ditch with a telegraph pole to sit on - which is quite revolting and may not come up to legally required standards; some may remember the sort of thing from scout camp days - to the grandeur of a complete bank of flushing lavatories in wooden cubicles sited within a lined marquee, complete with carpet and powder rooms. You need to get something which is suited to your event and finances. If you need a Public Entertainment Licence because you are running a largely musical event (see Chapter 16) the amount of sanitary facilities may be governed by the terms of the Licence.

Whatever you choose, try to make arrangements for wheel-chair visitors who cannot manage steps and there may be other special needs you want to cater for. I have yet to discover a mobile baby-change facility for hire but by the time this book gets into print perhaps one sympathetic manufacturer may have designed one. As mother of two small daughters I know that trying to change a squirming babe in the gloom, on your knee and in an area the size of a matchbox is no mean feat.

If your venue has a man-hole cover over a drain on site you will be able to use a mobile unit that has flushing facilities. This stands over the hole and drains direct into the main sewer. (In extremis they can drain directly into a deep hole dug for the purpose.) The flush is provided from a tank of water located in the roof. These mobile units are towed onto the site complete with a full tank, and left free standing. They are, very simply, a rectangular caravan with an internal division and a door at either end providing both male and female facilities in the one unit. The large mobile loos can probably accommodate four or five cubicles in the 'Ladies' and one cubicle and a six foot run of urinal in the 'Gents', both sides have handwashing facilities and some may be fitted with battery-powered lights. Arrangements have to be made to keep a supply of soap, paper and towels throughout the day.

The next best loo that you can use is a 'tardis' affair with one lavatory and a tiny basin in a rigid box. These come with and without a flush and use chemicals to sanitise the facility and should last the day, or more, without being topped up. The same system can be hired for less money if you go for a tent surround but this comes without the hand basin. You will need at least two of these single units.

Finally, and frankly only one stage better than the telegraph pole, a canvas surround is placed around a hole in the ground using a kind of shower base with a hole cut in the middle to provide 'croucho marks' - as one member of my family succinctly observed when describing French motorway facilities! Care must be taken when filling in these holes at the end of the day and a dose of lime might not go amiss.

You can hire all types of loos from builder's suppliers or marquee firms, the single units may be available from tool hire companies and your local council could either supply the larger units and disabled loos (sometimes free of charge) themselves or put you in touch with a supplier direct. The costs vary wildly from about £17 a day for the most basic, £55 per event (up to five days) for the full-flushing 'tardis' single unit, up to about £170 for a multi-user mobile trailer.

The law is rather open-ended about supplying toilet facilities for outdoor events. Legally, you are not obliged to supply any-thing unless it is within the terms of a Public Entertainments Licence as outlined above, but if you choose to do so - and you would be well advised to - you must supply facilities of a certain standard. Guidelines are available from your local Environmental Health Department and an Officer will always be prepared to advise you.

Very briefly, the figures that I always work to, based on a 4-6 hour show are as follows:

Female conveniences

1 WC per 150 females (100 if it is a family event)

Male conveniences

1 WC per 100 males

3 WCs per 500 males

5 WCs per 1,000 males

1.5m of urinal accommodation per 500 males

Unisex accommodation can allow greater flexibility and even a reduction in numbers of WCs, but you should increase mainte-nance supervision. You should increase provision if the event is longer than 6 hours duration.

10 CAR PARKING

For any event, be it indoors or out, in the country or in a big city you will have people arriving by car. This can be a good opportunity to make some extra money, although the added attraction of a free car park can swell the crowds. If you wish to control parking, due to a restricted area, you can just charge for car parking and have no entrance fee. This encourages more people to use one car and you can make your money in other ways on the site (see Chapter 6. under Marketing).

Any space that you do choose to use for a car park will have to offer a suitable surface. Parking on a beach, for instance, is unwise as cars may not be able to get out easily. Similarly, if you have had days of rain, the meadow that you had planned to use may be too boggy. On the other hand drivers do not expect acres of tarmacadam, beautifully marked out and most are prepared to park on grass and walk several hundred yards.

In a town or city you will not be able to make money from an official car park but parking will still have to be controlled, usually by the Police (see Chapter 5).

MAKING IT PAY

It is usual to charge for the car and not for the passengers. You will need to fence the area and allow only one entrance so that you can charge each car as it approaches. Frequently you can let the car park look after itself and open another access as a second exit after the first few hours as the small amount of cars coming towards the end of the show will not warrant keeping someone on the gate.

As long as it is fairly obvious where to park - placing a few staff cars in prominent places can help start the lines - or the field is very big you will not need stewards. If you are expecting a great many cars or think they will turn up all at once due to perhaps arriving in time for the start of a performance it might be prudent to have several stewards directing cars and taking money at the same time. In this way you can avoid a hold up in the road as they turn into the entrance.

JUST GETTING 'EM PARKED

As a rough guide, you need a 5m x 2m space to park one car and allow room for the passengers to get out without hitting the car next in line. If you have cars parked nose to nose with a 6m lane to use as a turning circle behind each double row you will not go far wrong. Coaches need a space 14m x 4m and you would be advised to keep them to a single line if possible, and separate from the cars.

It can help to reserve one section for cars with Passes even if you are not charging for parking. This ensures that the Mayor or other VIPs can find somewhere to park near to the entrance.

It isn't usually necessary to have marked and numbered spaces for small or medium scale events. These are only used if you are selling reserved spaces in advance.

The easiest way I know to get cars parked quickly and efficiently is to ask the Lions Club, Scouts (or similar) to help. You can usually arrange a mutually beneficial arrangement on the lines of: the Lions keep the car park money but supply stewards for the rest of the event; the event organisers keep the car park money but the Lions receive a percentage as a donation; or the organisers keep the money but allow the Lions some other money-making facility such as the tea-tent. Doing it this way takes the pressure off you; and clubs such as the Lions are experienced in controlling cars and very often have pre-printed bright vests to wear so it is clear who are the stewards. You do not have the added expense of having to hire white coats or print armbands.

If you are running an event where there are competitors or performers it is probably prudent to keep a separate area free for their vehicles. When it comes to horse boxes or stock lorries it is also a matter of safety to keep them away from the public. Look at the ground carefully if you expect large lorries. I remember one Summer when the river at the bottom of the competitors' car park had flooded the week before a Heavy Horse Show and although the ground seemed firm enough in the morning, by the end of the day trailer after trailer had difficulties getting off the park. One particularly heavy horse box eventually had to be towed out and I was not popular. Some trailers and lorries are very heavy!

It is possible that an event might finish after dark. This can present special security and safety problems that are not necessarily present during daylight. You may need to provide a few mobile floodlights so that pedestrians crossing the car park are not in danger and to deter thieves. Be very vigilant about trip hazards especially if bumbling pins and ropes are used to fence the park and make sure that the exits are clearly signed in direct light.

KEY POINTS

1 Decide if you want to make money from parking cars or not.

2 Estimate the amount of cars that may come and plan your area carefully and think about the surface. Don't forget to inform the Police.

3 Separate visitors' and competitors' or performers' cars.

4 Consider asking another organisation to organise the parking for you.

5 Light the area at night.

51

11 TIMESCALES AND CHECKLISTS

I have tried setting up events in various ways but the method that I always come back to in the end is working with a time table and a checklist. Things often take longer than you think and however much slack you build into the system invariably it runs out at the end. Events are no exception to the rule that 'work always expands to fit the time available'. But better too much time than not enough!

When I asked a fellow events organiser what his single most important piece of advice would be to a beginner planning an event, he replied 'allow yourself enough thinking time at the beginning' and he is quite right. But, how much is enough? First-timers often underestimate how long everything takes to arrange. You may put aside an afternoon to ring all the hire companies to get estimates for equipment, but what you forget is that the person you need to talk to may be out, or that the supplier who promises to call you back may fail to do so. You can waste literally hours on the telephone and it is frustrating if you are using your own domestic telephone and time off from work or the hour that the children are at nursery school.

The trouble with planning something months in advance, particularly if it is between glueing your own life together, going to work and looking after the kids, is that you tend to forget things. Checklists are vital and can help you out of a hole if you need to prove something was ordered or arranged if things go wrong.

I would never consider working without one and after many years I have perfected a very simple system that works for me. In this chapter I will explain the basic formula that I use to plan every event. It is only a guideline and you may well think you can do with less time or do things in a different order. But whatever way you chose, it is always a good idea to have thought things through in advance and to get some notes on paper so that someone else can understand your plans in an emergency.

Finally, time management is paper management! What do you do with all the paper that keeps accumulating once it is known that you are the event organiser? One thing is certain, if you ignore it or delay dealing with it you will lose vital information and waste time looking for things. On the way to a meeting and listening to Radio 4, I once heard a time management expert (I am ashamed to say that his name escapes me) going through the junk on the programme presenter's desk. His code impressed me deeply and I still work to the following rules.

'When faced with a piece of paper there is one of four things that you should do immediately:

   a. Act on it

   b. File it

   c. Pass it on

   d. Bin it

and lo and behold you have a tidy desk and no nasty jobs waiting for your attention!'

TIME MANAGEMENT

There are books and books on this subject so I don't intend to go into great detail here. However there are tricks to manage your time efficiently and I hope that by the end of this chapter to have increased your confidence and show you how you can break up your tasks into manageable chunks. The simplest form of a time management chart is a calendar and my timetable is really just that but it is intended to be used alongside a checklist.

There are really only two types of task that you undertake when you plan an event. I use my check list for the first and my wall planner or time table for the second.

1. Instant or easily completed jobs e.g. Booking the caterers, arranging to have chairs delivered, or inviting the Lord Mayor to open the show.

2. Continuous or on-going jobs e.g. Marketing, public relations, or pre-event workshops.

But before you do anything you must make four decisions:

1. What the event is

2. Where it is to be held

3. When it is to be held

4. Who will run it or be the main contact and where all the correspondence is to be sent; 'the registered office' as it were.

Some or all of this will have been decided by a committee but delegated powers will have to be given to the main contact so that quick decisions can be effected. In general committee-led events need more time to set up than the 'one man band'. On the other hand, for a large or complicated show, it is impossible to do everything yourself and a committee is not only useful but vital - so horses for courses as the saying goes. (See Chapter 4 on Committees).

PLANNERS

For every event, with no exception, I use the definitive checklist (there is a copy of this for you to photocopy at the back of the book). This often has items that are irrelevant for a particular show but, no problem, I just put a line through them and at least I have remembered them. Just occasionally there is an item that is peculiar to just one event and I have a space available to add this.

The next steps could not be easier: **A:** When first taking over the organisation, go through the entire numbered checklist and write the number on the wall chart next to the date that you need to start thinking about a particular item. **B:** As you order or make arrangements for each element mark the date that you dealt with it in the first column on the checklist. **C:** Finally, as you receive confirmation or collect the item itself, write this new date in the second column. **D:** A third column is left clear for you to add special comments or the telephone no. or address of the person to whom you have delegated that particular job.

Then comes the wall chart and this is where you need some discipline and sometimes strict self-motivation. These tasks are more abstract and it is easy to put them off for a day when you have more time, energy or whatever. Don't! At least set them in motion when you need to; put the ball in someone else's court and you will be amazed at what you can achieve. **A:** Work out your marketing plan, decide about programmes, tickets, advertising, promotions etc, make your own publicity checklist (there is a sample at the back of the book). **B:** Very early on arrange meetings with the media, printers and start attracting sponsors if necessary. **C:** As a result of the meetings mark on your wall chart (I find Sasco make an excellent range) when they need copy, art work, further meetings, interviews, etc. **D:** Make a note of dates when you may need to follow up tenuous interest. **E:** Some things can go on your checklist as before, such as printing tickets, collecting programmes, even paying in advance for press ads.

Use the following as a rough timescale for your major tasks:

- Decide on the type of event and the date 9-12 months ahead.
- Form your committee at the very start or at least 9 months ahead.
- Start looking for sponsors if you need them 9-12 months ahead: longer, if your event is a big one.
- Inform your Local Authority 6-12 months ahead for advice, information and possible grants.
- Book the venue 6-12 months ahead.
- Book major acts 9-12 months ahead, non-headliners can wait until 6 months.
- Inform Tourist Information Centres, event listings or specialist publications 6-12 months ahead.
- At least check on availability of infrastructure if outdoors or lighting/sound equipment if indoors 6-9 months ahead. Book as soon as you are certain what you will need.
- Send a press release to the local media as soon as you firm up on date, venue, benefiting charity etc.
- Book first aid, caterers, judges, comperes, Mayor and other services 6-9 months ahead.
- Send out competitors' schedules 4-6 months ahead.
- Start looking for volunteers 3-4 months ahead. You can try earlier but people book holidays, have Aunty Mildred to stay or just forget if you organise help too soon.
- Talk about finances very early in the proceedings. You can delay opening an account until you have some money (or need to spend some) but do it by about 2-3 months ahead.
- Order publicity material 3 months ahead, send it out 6-8 weeks in advance. Any earlier than this and posters will be covered up and people will have forgotten your event all together. You could book your print run in at the printers earlier if you wish to be sure of not being pushed aside by another job.
- Apply for licences at the appropriate times (see Chapter 16): at least start thinking about them 3-4 months ahead.
- Notify the Police at least 4 weeks in advance or 3 months if you know your event will have serious traffic implications or you require a Liquor licence.
- Hold a final meeting 1 week ahead.
- You could hold a stewards/ushers/money-handlers briefing 3-5 days ahead.
- Get some rest the night before!

▶▶ BILL'S PROGRESS

This may be a good opportunity to visit the Dog Show committee again and see what stage Bill Pincher has reached with his show.

Bill first thought of his idea way back in October. The committee was formed at Christmas time, they had their first meeting on 13 January and have arranged to meet every second Wednesday of the month in a private room of the 'Bowl and Whistle'. They decided to hold the dog show on Sunday 9 July as it is the last weekend before the schools break-up for the Summer holidays. It is now the middle of May and Bill's list looks like this (the dates of order and confirmation have been omitted):

EVENT: Exemption Dog Show and Canine Care Day

DATE: 9 July **TIME:** 10.30am - 4.30pm
VENUE: Brick Close Com   munity Centre and recreation ground, Goridge, East Anglia
ADMN: £1.50 **CONCESSIONS:** £1.00 OAP, Children 5-12, UB40, disabled; children under 5 Free
CAR PARK: Playing field **CHARGE:** No charge

---

1. **CONTACT:** Promotions officer, Goridge Town council **TEL:** 543221
   Community Centre caretaker - Hector Hogg **Tel:** 36801

---

2. **HIRE FEE:** £150 due 1 week prior
3. **DEPOSIT:** £50 (paid)
4. **MARQUEE:** Allweather tents Ltd x2
   FEE: £40x2 C.O.D.
5. **PAYGATE:** Trestle Tables from Community Centre (gratis)
6. **FENCING:** Not needed, already fenced
7. **CATERERS:** Girl Guides
8. **WATER:** Outside tap from Community Centre
9. **ELECTRICITY:** From Community Centre
10. **LIGHTING:** None
11. **REFUSE:** Skip from Binman Ltd
    FEE: £30 (payable in advance)
    8 x Tuff-Tubs and liners from Council (gratis)

12. **P.A.:** Loudsound Bros. £150 (will be invoiced)
13. **CHAIRS:** Truck + driver from Red Tile Co. collect 150 chairs from St. Martin's Church Hall, 8.30am deliver to Community Centre, reverse 5.30pm (gratis)
14. **VEHICLE ACCESS:** From Tilehouse Road
15. **SCHOOL:** Mr. Ruler (Headteacher) to arrange Parade and painting competition
15. **CHURCH:** Advised Rev. Saintly (watch for wedding cars at 3.30pm)
16. **INSURANCE:** Public Liability - Cornhill £35 All risks - £25 (paid)
17. **FIRE PREVENTION:** 2 x Extinguishers (Community Centre + Tea Tent)
18. **FIRE BRIGADE:** Not necessary
19. **AMBULANCE:** Not necessary
20. **POLICE:** Notified (meeting on site 2 weeks before)
21. **SECURITY:** 6 x Cash collectors; Mary Malone, Dick Tracy, Herbert Greenback, George Clink, Susan and Gordon Gold
22. **FIRST AID:** Red Cross
23. **VET:** Alan from RSPCA
24. **COLLECTION LICENCE:** Applied for from Town Hall
25. **FLOAT MONEY/WAGES:** Gordon to arrange
26. **BANK:** Barclays, High Street
27. **ACTS:** John Copper with Victor to arrive 12.00 for 12.30pm & 3.00pm School Parade to arrive 9.30am for 10.00am
28. **COMPETITION:** Rufus Byte from Calamity Kennels to arrange. First competitors arrive 9.30am for 10.30am
29. **JUDGE:** Mrs. Daphne Furry arrive 10.00am
30. **STEWARDS:** Alison Beck, Julia Call
31. **EXHIBITION:** RSPCA to arrange, collect Friday am
32. **STALLS:** Arthur Pint from 'The Bowl and Whistle' to arrange, 20 stands and fast food vehicles arrive from 8.30am
33. **CIVIC DIGNITARIES:** Mayor arrives 3.00pm, presents cup 4.00pm
34. **SPECIAL ARRANGEMENTS:** Film Projector to be collected from Art School, Friday pm. Film from Tooth and Claw Film Co. arrive BR Red Star Wed pm (will ring when ready for collection). Projectionist - Olivia Knight
35. **POSTERS:** Inkpen Studios
36. **PRESS ADS:** Goridge Evening News, Tilehouse Citizen, What's On in Town. (will invoice) RSPCA Newsletter (Gratis)

12 BUDGETING

Some people are drawn to figure work, budgeting or indeed anything to do to with money as cats are to cream. They lap it up and thrive on every chink of coin or crumple of note. I am not one! This area of work is my 'bete noir', and because I do not enjoy mathematics my budget sheets are as simple as possible. In my opinion, even for the most grand of events, nothing more is needed than two columns for estimated income and expenditure and two for actuals with room to balance it at the bottom. All this can be written up simply on balance sheet paper obtainable from any stationers.

The most difficult part of any budget is estimating your income. As with a new product or a young company it is tempting to wildly overestimate due to your own enthusiasm. I always work to the ceiling of 50% capacity for any inside event or 40% for an outdoor show. This means that you have built in potentially damaging factors that are out of your control such as weather, competition or just plain apathy. These figures are not written in tablets of stone, and as the date approaches and it becomes clear that you are going to do better - by looking at pre-date ticket sales or extra interest from the media - then you can continuously adjust your estimated balance.

If a large part of your income is going to be from sponsorship or donations then you will have to ensure that they will be forthcoming before you get very far down the line. At least basic expenditure must be met otherwise you will find that you are paying for a costly mistake out of club funds or even worse, out of your own pocket.

OBTAINING ESTIMATES/QUOTATIONS

Try to obtain a quotation for everything and failing that, at least an estimate. A quotation is a legally binding document and it 'quotes' the exact figure that you will be charged; an estimate is only an informed guess and if they make a mistake in judging the job accurately you could find yourself with a larger bill than you expected. If you have enough time, your committee should agree large items of expenditure if they have not already set a budget. Setting a budget is fine in theory and if you have had a little experience, but if this is your first event you would do better to obtain as many estimates as you can and then hold a special meeting to talk about how you are going to spend your precious cash. There will be a lot of arguments but at least you can thrash out some sort of consensus and you, the organiser, will not be accused of being profligate if the profits are not as high as planned.

NEGOTIATING

All things are worth negotiating for; as mentioned in Chapter 7 times are hard, competition is tough and it is a buyer's market. Printers are a good example of companies that are worth negotiating with (see Chapter 6 under the section on Print and Design).

Remember that you expect a captive audience and so have a good bargaining hand. Most companies need to advertise and you may be able to obtain services or equipment free of charge in return for flying a company banner around the show ring or giving a credit in the programme. If you are looking for a media launch of a 'season' or a 'festival' it is worth looking for a sponsor to provide the refreshments and even the venue (more about serious full sponsorship in Chapter 14).

SCROUNGING

Some small, privately owned companies may have a director who is interested in your particular charity and is prepared to help purely out of sympathy for the cause - but these are few and far between.

If you are looking for equipment or facilities to be lent free of charge you may well find them offered, once. I feel that is not politic to keep going back to the same people year after year unless they make it very plain that they want to assist annually. However, for those who really do want to be associated with the event and enjoy the whole razz-a-matazz, it can help cement a good relationship to stick with the same donor year after year. A small 'thank you' present goes down well and only needs to be a bunch of flowers or even a free ticket. People are very generous where small events are concerned, especially in the more rural parts of the country; you may have to work a little harder in urban areas but you very often will have a more responsive council to work with.

● ● ● ● ● ● ● ● ● ●

KEY POINTS

① Use a simple accounting system

② Estimate your expenses carefully, allowing a wide margin for problems

③ Make sure that basic expenditure can be met

④ Obtain sponsorship and donations early on

⑤ Ask for 'quotes' as far as possible

⑥ Discuss major expenditure with your committee

⑦ Negotiate over everything

⑧ Remember to send a 'thank you' for help

⑨ Use your local Radio station for difficult items

⑩ Use local magazines

⑪ Open a bank account at least two weeks before you need it or warn a local bank that you would like to bank all the takings on a particular date.

If you are desperate for an expensive or unusual item that you cannot find through the usual channels, your local Radio station may come up trumps. They are often happy to give out any requests on air provided the event is not for personal gain and of course the person or company able to help gets a good plug too.

Church or parochial magazines are a good market place for requests for volunteers and equipment as well as advertising for the actual show. Remember, though, that they are often quarterly and will need copy well in advance.

KEEPING TRACK OF THE PENNIES

If you are holding a small event in connection with an established club then you will be able to use the club's bank account and cheque books (signed by the appropriate person, of course). But maybe your event, like the Dog Show, is a one-off. You will need to open a separate account with one of the main clearing banks which are, in the main, sympathetic towards charity events and could well grant you free banking for the first 3 - 12 months. Alternatively the correct Building Society account can be a good bet, as these do not incur costs.

In theory you can walk into any bank or building society and open an account within about twenty minutes, but in practice you will need to allow about two weeks before you can start using the account to ensure that cheque books are printed and available and that the account is fully up and running. If you think your event will become an annual show it is left to the discretion of each branch manager to decide if you need to open a new account each year, or if you can leave the present account dormant and then revive it for the three or four months of each year that you need to use it.

If your event is very low-key and all you need is a facility to bank the income then the Bank will be happy to use one of it's sundry accounts and issue a cheque to the charity or organisation. Clearly this could be used as way to 'launder' ill-gotten gains so the Bank will insist that a person, preferably an account holder, who is known to them presents the money. Generally a charge - around £10 - is made for this service but most Banks are prepared to waive the fee if it is known that the money is for fundraising.

▶▶ BILL'S PROGRESS

Herbert Greenback is the Committee's Treasurer. He lives on the Brick Close estate with his parents and four younger brothers and a sister. Aged 26 he has been drinking in Arthur's pub for a good few years and Bill always thought he was a bit fly. Molly said he was 'so sharp he'd cut hisself'. Though still fond of the odd crazy-coloured shirt, Bill had to admit that after Herb came back from London and applied himself to the course at the Gorridge Tech he really seemed to have changed. Now he works for one of the most respected firm of accountants in the area and is looking forward to taking his final exams in the Summer. Bill respects his judgement and the committee have listened to his advice with interest.

Since they have never attempted any event before, the committee asked the RSPCA to handle the money side of things. The charity agreed to allow the local office to oversee the event and gave autonomy to Bill's Superior Officer, but the event had to be run as a part of the RSPCA's activities. This meant that the event automatically had charitable status and a reputable name to use when hiring or ordering facilities and services.

On the down side, Bill is disappointed that 'his' event doesn't seem to be 'his' any longer; he also has to take any bills that need paying to his boss so that he can sign the cheques. Bill was all for accepting his superior's suggestion that he should be the signee of a separate RSPCA account but at the next meeting Herb pointed out that Bill's boss would be able to sanction any overspends that might be necessary thus giving them the equivalent of a free overdraft facility.

Afterwards Herb asked Bill to help him carry fish and chips home for all his family. On the way, and in between the odd chip, he made it clear to Bill that at this stage it was better to accept the very generous offer of the RSPCA to, in effect, guarantee any losses. If the Dog Day was to be repeated in future years that might be the time to have their own account - especially if they made a profit this year. He explained that if they did well they should keep £100 back, having at first agreed it with the RSPCA, to put on deposit and provide a float for next year's expenses. They would be able to trade off the reputation gained this year and hopefully still have the charity's blessing to fundraise in their name. They would also be free to fundraise for other causes in addition.

13 TICKET SALES AND KEEPING YOUR MONEY SAFE

Not all events make money through selling tickets, but it is the traditional way of selling indoor events and a large proportion of outdoor shows are also 'tickets only'. But what system should you use and how do you keep track of the sales?

Selling tickets may be one of your main aims in putting on a fundraising event but having lots of cash rattling around and often at a weekend, can be a major headache. Security actually during the course of your event is dealt with in Chapter 19, but after the event is over you will want to be sure that your precious profits are safe until the banks open. As has been stressed all through this guide, every event is different and has unique needs but in this chapter we will look at some of the most popular methods of selling tickets and looking after the resulting cash. There is also a quick word about VAT.

IDEAS FOR SELLING TICKETS
You can sell a ticket in two different ways; days or even weeks prior to an event or on the door as people actually arrive for the show itself. It is rare that an outdoor event has tickets in advance but a large proportion of indoor shows are sold in this way. There are advantages and disadvantages in both methods and you will need to work out your own needs and situation to choose which is best for your event.

ADVANCE SALES
The advantages
a. You have a longer time in which to sell the tickets
b. Money is paid in advance
c. You can control sales for a limited space
d. You can make decisions based on real sales and not just on predicted sales
e. If you 'sell out' in advance you can avoid queues of disappointed customers being turned away

f. It is usually easier to keep track of advance tickets and money as you have smaller quantities to deal with
g. You can make tickets available to the convenience of your audience and allow them to buy them when the mood is upon them i.e. NOW!

The disadvantages

a. You need to have someone available to sell tickets for a lengthy period, although you can use an Answerphone.
b. You need to make frequent arrangements to collect and bank money and an account to deposit it
c. You need one or more separate selling points if you are not using mail order only
d. You need to print official tickets
e. Tickets can be copied and sold illegally

SELLING TICKETS ON THE GATE

The advantages

a. You only need ticket sellers for a limited period
b. You can use preprinted raffle tickets or in some cases no tickets at all
c. You can control entry to known trouble makers
d. There are no arguments about losing tickets etc.

The disadvantages

a. You may have a long and at times impatient queue
b. You will have to cope with large amounts of cash
c. It can be hard to keep track of sales
d. Concessions are very often given on trust. It is impractical to check UB40s or pension books in front of a swiftly moving queue

Having decided how you are to sell your show you will now need to decide if you need tickets at all and if so, what they should be. In my opinion you do need to have some sort of record of sales for every event, even if you are collecting 10p at the door for a Village Hall Jumble Sale. Cloakroom or raffle tickets are ideal for this sort of event and they are often all you need for a ticketed outdoor show. Each ticket has a separate security number as well as being sequentially numbered and are available in rolls or books of many different colours. You can have several entrances controlled by different colours which enables you to have a record of gate

KEY POINTS

1 Decide if you will charge for admission

2 Study the advantages and disadvantages for the two methods of selling tickets

3 Ensure that you keep a record of sales

4 Choose advance ticket sales outlets that are in keeping with the show

5 Ensure that cash is removed regularly when selling tickets on the day

6 Try to make arrangements so that you never have to take money home. Use the night safe at your bank if at all possible

7 Decide if you will be liable for V.A.T; if so you must be registered

popularity. You can reserve one colour especially for car parking, OAPs, families, people using wheelchairs or any group that you wish to research for future reference.

Advance sales are rather different and need to be 'official', by this I mean pre-printed onto books or rolls. These tickets should also be security numbered to deter counterfeiters especially for popular shows and there are specialist printers who will do this for you, such as Ticketshop in Reading who can provide tickets nationally. (Address at the back of the book).

The ticket should show the name of the show, the date, the price paid, and the seat number if necessary. It is also helpful if a telephone number is given for any enquiries. I favour tickets in books as you can keep the stubs all together and give different books to each selling point. This also helps when it comes to reconciling the sales over a period of weeks.

If you are selling tickets for a one-off fundraising show you will not have permanent box-office facilities unless you are using a purpose built theatre. You will need to arrange a ticket outlet and advertise it well.

The simplest way to sell tickets in advance is by mail on receipt of a cheque or postal order. You can then do away with the need to staff a sales point.

A shop or pub is a good place to sell tickets from especially if the owners are contributing to the show by sponsorship or providing the bar. Your local Tourist Information Centre might be prepared to sell tickets on commission as might your Council especially if the event is held on Council property. Bookshops are often happy to be associated with arts events and the Chamber of Commerce might help with a trade show. Try to choose an outlet that is related to the type of event, not only are they more likely to assist but you will mutually benefit from like customers.

OTHER FORMS OF INCOME INCLUDING TRADE STANDS

You can make money by selling programmes, games stalls, balloon races, raffle tickets (see Chapter 16 on the Lotteries Act), or merchandising direct to the general public; you will find a list of companies who can provide entire fundraising packages at the back of the book. You can also sell trade stand plots. This can be very profitable and popular - sometimes it is a job to get them to stop coming in! £25 - £40 a site is the going rate at the time of going to press but this very much depends on the size and flavour of your event. Because of the state of the economy many workers who have been made redundant have taken their hand-out and started a mobile trade stand. There are now many more traders than one event could ever use and plots need to be advertised well in advance. Decide how many you want - sometimes even limiting the types, such as 5 fast food, 2 plant or 3 sweet vans - and collect the plot fee a couple of weeks prior to the event. On a bad day it can be very difficult to get your money if you have arranged to collect at the gate. Never charge a percentage of their take as there is no reliable way of checking it and even if you could it is too time consuming.

COLLECTING CASH AND KEEPING IT SAFE

Unless you have a till you will need something to keep your float and sales money in. At the very least a couple of empty ice cream containers will do. Keep them fitted one inside the other with notes in the bottom one so that they do not blow away. Two people are needed on the door, one to tear off tickets and keep an eye on the queue and one to look after the money and give change. If one is called away in an emergency you will still have someone to sell tickets.

For larger outside events you will need several people along a six foot table for every entrance or filter that you are using. You should keep money in several containers to prevent losing the lot if someone makes a grab for it. Ensure that a couple of trustworthy collectors are appointed to remove the paper money at regular intervals throughout the day. They will need somewhere secure to take it to and a safe kept in a staffed club caravan or clubhouse is ideal.

After the event is over the bank or building society may not be open for you to deposit the income. You will need to have access to a safe or make arrangements with your bank to use the night-safe, preferably during the hours of daylight. It is probably unwise to take the money home unless it really is a very small amount. On the Monday morning give the Bank or Building Society a telephone call to warn them that you are coming in and give them an indication as to how much you think you are bringing. They may want you to come at a time when they know they will be quiet as one cashier will be busy counting your money for some time especially if you have had a collection in small coins. (See Chapter 12 for opening an account.)

VAT

If your turnover is small, then you will be below the VAT registration threshold (currently £35,100 annual turnover; not net profit), even when the event income is not exempt. This means that if your income for the year excluding donations is less than the registration threshold, then you will not need to worry about VAT.

As a general rule of thumb, VAT is charged on all tickets sold for personal gain or as part of a going concern such as a Rock concert company or Theatre. One-off or annual fundraising events are usually exempt from VAT apart from those which are part of a series and for which you can obtain season or discounted tickets. If your one-off events, albeit for charity, are held in the same place as often as once a month you will be liable for VAT as it is felt that the charity is now taking trade from commercial organisations and has an unfair tax advantage.

Coffee mornings and jumble sales, however, can be held every week and in the same hall if desired without being accountable for VAT as the risk of competition is thought to be marginal.

A two or three day event for which there is one admission charge is exempt from paying VAT, but an event taking place over a weekend where an entrance fee is charged on both Saturday and Sunday will be taxed.

If you wish to learn more about the details of Charity VAT exemptions there is a very clear pamphlet available (VAT leaflet 701/1/92) from HM Customs and Excise Office.

14 SPONSORSHIP AND GRANTS

The pot from which money used to be relatively freely distributed is emptying fast. There are more hands trying to get into the pot and less money available in the beginning. Central government used to make payments direct to some charitable projects. The NHS frequently has to find charitable funding for equipment and services that were once available from government sources, and companies that were once happy to be associated with cultural or charitable projects have had to withdraw due to the longest recession in recent history or have had their fingers burnt in the past, perhaps because they have been perceived to be associated with an unfashionable activity (e.g. boxing or beauty contests). The result is that the few sources that are still functioning are heavily oversubscribed.

WHERE TO GO FOR HELP

For small and medium-scale events it is unlikely that you will want to apply for a grant of more than a few hundred or, at the absolute outside, a couple of thousand pounds. Some Local Authorities are still keeping a small budget for community events or shows that they think will attract tourists into the area or which meet a local community need. It is worth applying well in advance or seeing the council's Promotions' Officer to find out what is available (see Chapter 5) but you will need to make a professional looking application. There are some very good publications on this subject and on company sponsorship listed at the back of the book.

If you are not successful then you are perfectly justified to know why, so ask what it was that they didn't like about your application. It may be that the budget was just so small and the demands so many that the line had to be drawn somewhere, even on a first come first served basis. So get in quick!

There are other sources of grants and these could include local trusts, funds from educational bodies or other quasi-governmental help (see the back of the book for some helpful directories on this subject, and below). The ITV Television Company usually will make a large number of small grants available for local events within their franchise region. Whether we can expect this practice to continue after the new franchises come into force has yet to be seen. But there are those who think it will.

WHAT YOU CAN OFFER THEM

Where sponsorship is sought from companies, industry or organisations you are usually expected to be able to offer something in return. It often helps to be able to ask for a specific project, such as a media launch or prizes rather than a general donation into the kitty. This is usually more newsworthy and they can get a photograph in the local paper and their house magazine with a good paragraph of promotional spiel. (There is more of this in Chapter 6 in the section on Marketing).

The most obvious thing that you can offer in return for sponsorship is 'corporate identity' or awareness, by which I mean allowing all your publicity to bear the name, logo or 'house colours' of your sponsors which helps the company to become a recognised, household name. Be aware that your sponsors might wish to flood the event with company publicity and you may wish to limit this. Make sure that you know what the event is worth to them in terms of advertising and don't sell yourselves short.

You could allow banners around show rings or around entrances. The programmes and prizes can bear the company logo. At staged events every member of the audience could even receive a pack about a particular service that is offered by the sponsors. You may wish to hold a reception for specially invited guests prior to the event for company VIPs or prestige customers or even a special showing, all to be paid for, of course, by the sponsors. Ask what they would like and other extras they are prepared to pay for, and make sure that you are all in agreement.

PRESENTING YOUR CASE

Because of the difficulties of obtaining sponsorship in the last few years you will need to be very professional in conducting your argument and if this is to be your main form of funding you would be well advised to start early and take very good advice. I have neither the space nor the expertise to recommend a course of action here but there are some helpful publications listed at the end of the book.

15 INSURANCE

It is most irresponsible to run an event or show without Public Liability Insurance cover. By far and away the most popular events in the UK during the Summer months are Fetes and Car Boot Sales and even the smallest of school fetes or most insignificant of sales should be insured. You might just get away with ignoring a coffee morning in the Vicarage garden but even then a hot water urn can blow up or a garden seat collapse and you could be liable if anything like this happens. Public Liability insurance covers you from claims made by people who can prove that their accident or injury was as a direct result of the event organiser's negligence. If they suffer as a result of not taking reasonable care for their own safety there is no claim or the responsibility may be shared.

You are not required by law to take out insurance cover but for a really very small premium (£20+ minimum) you could save yourself or your club from a crippling financial burden.

There are many, many companies that claim to provide insurance cover for small and medium scale events but they are often very specialised or need answers to so many questions that it can be quite daunting for the beginner who only wants cover for a small village fair.

I have found Cornhill Insurance a very good all round insurance company who are prepared to provide cover for all types of shows. The proposal forms are very clear and logical and they divide the types of events into three groups to facilitate a quick decision. You can expect to pay a £22 premium (1992) on an indemnity limit of £500,000 for a one day event in Group A such as a Pet Show or Street Party. A Traction Engine Rally or County Show running over one week would classify as Group C and the premium is still modest at £190 for an indemnity limit of £1,000,000.

In addition to Public Liability you can look at cover for other areas such as Rainfall. Cornhill Insurance will provide this as will Eagle Star, but again I would go for Cornhill as, and I quote one insurance broker, Eagle Star need so much detail that they would ask your shoe size if you let them! Rainfall cover will pay your fixed costs i.e. hiring charges, labour costs, publicity etc. (the premium is calculated as a percentage of the Public Liability quotes) should your event be cancelled because of rain, hail or snow within 24 hours before the start of the show.

The third form of popular cover is All Risks, Money and Personal Assault. This covers damage or theft to property associated with the event, theft of money and attack on volunteers, helpers and other organisers. The premium is (1992) a flat fee of £25 or £40 for property worth up to £5,000 and £10,000 respectively.

For more unique events it is worth investigating companies that specialise in certain areas. Norwich Union provide excellent cover for Art Exhibitions and have a purpose-built package that covers exhibits in transit as well as the show itself which is most convenient. I have also used Norwich Union for Horse Shows and Street Processions and they would probably be prepared to provide a tailor-made package for anything unusual. Broad Street Insurance specialise in Model Railway Club Exhibitions and Stamp Insurance Services clearly cover exhibitions organised by Stamp Societies. Jackson Emms Insurance Group have a valuable service covering all aspects of weddings and the Prudential Assurance Company will cover all sorts of events but are thought to be especially suited to music festivals and concerts.

For any event, unless you are absolutely certain what you require and who can provide it, it is probably safer to use a broker to advise you. They can guide you through the sections on the proposal form and ensure that it is completed accurately. If there are any claims the broker will also be able to take some of the anxiety out of the situation.

16 LICENCES, BYE-LAWS AND BOOZE

It is probably true to say that most events contravene the strict letter of the law in one way or another. However, most of the time the areas of contravention are so uncertain that in general if the event isn't dangerous, causing a nuisance and there are no complaints then the authorities tend to turn a blind eye. The thinking is that it is a one-off and by the time the fuss has been made everything is all over anyway. The exception is where there could be danger to the public.

Laws are made to ensure that the general public are not put at risk in any way and that basic rights are not overturned. If you have these two fundamental areas in the back of your mind when you set up your events you will not go far wrong.

However there is no built-in tolerance factor for certain activities and you will need to apply for a licence before you start. A Liquor Licence when selling alcohol is mandatory as is an Entertainments Licence if you are organising an event where music or dancing is the main attraction. Raffles and gambling games must comply with the Lotteries Act. Other laws are more flexible being under the discretion of the enforcing authority e.g. Sunday Trading Laws, Street Collection Permits and local bye-laws.

In the following sections I will try to explain each in detail to enable you to make an informed decision as to what licence, if any, that you will need. I, however, am not a lawyer and the rules are frequently subject to revision so whilst I have done my best to simplify and point out the most relevant parts of the law, please take specialised advice if you are in any doubt. You only need to telephone the appropriate licensing authority to make absolutely sure. Food Hygiene laws and guidelines are dealt with separately in Chapter 25.

PUBLIC ENTERTAINMENT LICENCES

The law (Local Government, Miscellaneous Provisions, Act 1982) states that where two or more people are performing and/or dancing is involved, a Public Entertainments Licence is required. The main areas of concern are the safety of the electrical system, any potential fire hazards and the availability of fire escapes, exits and procedures for emptying the building, and noise pollution. Inside and outside events may be treated rather differently but the concerns will not change.

Shows that include a hypnotism act may be banned or restricted in certain Local Authority areas; it is worth getting advice if you are hiring a council owned venue as inclusion could affect granting a licence.

1. Inside events:

These tend to be potentially more hazardous when held in a previously unlicensed building. If, however, you have chosen a public building in which to hold your event such as a Church Hall, pub or Community centre then you may well find that the building already holds a Public Entertainments Licence and all you have to do is comply with the terms previously agreed. For something like a Ceildh held in the local farmer's barn or a concert in the village church a temporary Public Entertainments Licence will have to be sought. You will need to apply at least three months in advance to allow time for resubmission if you are at first unsuccessful.

Do not even think of applying if you can not guarantee several fire exits or if your venue backs on to a noise sensitive building such as a hospital or sheltered accommodation.

2. Outside events:

Generally speaking if musical entertainment is not the main attraction, the authorities are not really interested. If you are expecting a crowd of more than a few hundred people it might be prudent to take advice should you be planning a DJ and disco as part of the fun; it is just possible that in urban areas complaints will have been made before and the Environmental Protection Officers may be more sensitive than usual.

If you plan an event to comprise largely of performers you will certainly have to apply for a Public Entertainments Licence and, as for inside events, plan to apply for this at least three months in advance.

PROCEDURE FOR APPLYING FOR
A PUBLIC ENTERTAINMENTS LICENCE

A: Visit the Local Authority relevant to the area in which you plan to hold the event. Ask to see someone from the Licensing Section of the Administration Department or make an appointment.

B: You will be given several copies (at least 5 or 6) of a form on which you should specify the type of licence that you require - usually music and dancing. The Enforcement Officer should be happy to advise you. You will also be asked to give the name and address of the venue and your (the applicant's) name and address and a plan of the building or site that you intend to use. There may also be a space to add the date of the licensing committee that you wish to consider the application. There will be a charge of between £100 and £200 depending on the Authority.

C: The copies are sent variously to the Chief Fire Officer, the Police, the Environmental Health Department and the remainder to the Licensing Officer.

D: You will also be asked to submit an electrical certificate, perhaps separately to the Environmental Health Department. This is usually arranged and paid for by the promoter and can be quite expensive according to the size of the building or rig used. At the time of writing (1992) £150+ is the going rate. The inspection must be carried out by a qualified electrician and one who is approved by the licensing authority so make sure that you do your homework first.

E: Then comes the wait. Before the committee hears your application you may well have a visit from one or more of the interested bodies to hear about your event in more detail. If your event is outside you will be unable to supply certain information or an electrical certificate as the infrastructure will not be in place - so expect a decision to be made with conditions.

F: You may well be ordered to advertise the date and nature of the event in the local press and by poster outside your proposed venue (at your own expense). This is to enable potential complainants to come forward to have their comments taken into consideration when the committee meets.

G: If your application is successful you can proceed according to plan. If the application is successful but conditions are imposed you will have to show that these can be met - often on the day of the event - and an officer will make arrangements to inspect just hours before you open to the public. S/he has the right to prevent the show from opening or restrict part of it, although in practice, it is unlikely that this will happen if your venue is not actively dangerous.

LIQUOR LICENCES

If you wish to sell alcohol, or intoxicating liquor as it is legally called, at your event you will have to be licensed. The decision to grant a licence is made by the local Magistrates Court who take advice from the Police. If you are holding a show in a building that already has a licensed bar then provided that the licensee is in charge of his bar during the event you will have no problems.

Outside, or in an unlicensed building, it is a different matter and it very rare that a complete stranger to the licensed trade is granted a temporary liquor licence. To be sure of obtaining permission to open your bar you should approach a licensee who already holds a full 'on-licence' and ask him/her to apply for you. This is quite legal and indeed the Police welcome this action as the landlord is, in effect, asking to extend the area of his/her pub for the duration of the event. Having found your tame landlord, the procedure is as follows:

PROCEDURE FOR APPLYING FOR A LIQUOR LICENCE

A: The licensee applies to the Magistrates Court, giving details of the event itself, the venue and what area is to covered by the licence. (This could be just the immediate bar area or include a fenced off seating area outside a tent). S/he will be required to give one month's notice, although in practice, if you are desperate for a licence your Court may well be able to give you a decision within 48 hours.

B: You will be given 3 copies of the application form one of which has to sent to the Police, so that they have a chance to object. The other two are returned to the Court.

C: Most Courts have a sitting twice a week to decide on licences and you should be informed fairly promptly by letter as to which way the hearing went. If your event is less than one month from the sitting you will be asked to attend the hearing so you will know the decision instantly. Incidentally, if you fail to show up at the court when you have specifically been asked to attend your application may automatically be turned down.

D: In some cases the Police will not recommend refusal of the licence but they might put restrictions on it. For instance the Lord Mayor's Street Procession in Norwich has traditionally been granted a licence for a beer tent in the city centre gardens but in recent years this has been the site of rowdiness and under-age drinking and the Police have imposed conditions to try and limit these problems. The licensee has had to agree to all alcohol being sold in open disposable 'glasses' (so that tins cannot be passed to under-age consumers) and the beer tent had to have an area fenced off to prevent drink being consumed elsewhere in the park; a full hour has also been knocked off the opening times. This was not a popular decision but has, nevertheless, helped to solve the problems.

STREET COLLECTION PERMITS

One very effective method of fundraising is to organise a collection or a flag day. Usually these are held in the main shopping streets of towns and cities but they can be just as productive when held on site during the course of an event.

You are not, however, allowed to organise a collection when and wherever you feel like it unless it is on private property when you will, of course, have to gain permission from the owner. There is considerable scope for collecting within private buildings and these can include private houses, cinemas, pubs, theatres, club houses, railways and underground stations or even the steps of churches or frontages of shops and stores. Collections can also be made without a permit at an open air meeting but you will be required to obtain permission from the Local Authority to actually hold the meeting.

The Local Government Act, 1972 gives powers to Local Authorities to regulate collections on public property and details may vary slightly around the country. The Charities Act 1992 has tightened these regulations further and you will be required to apply, in writing, to the Administration Department of the Council covering the area in which the collection is to be held at least one month prior to the event, and possibly a great deal earlier than that if you want to be sure of booking the day you need.

GETTING A STREET COLLECTION PERMIT

Generally, the basis on which a permit is granted is as follows:

A: Only one organisation to collect each day and that group must only collect on the allotted day and between the times as stated on the permit and in the permitted place. (The permitted place may be the whole of the town centre or it could be restricted to just one street).

B: People carrying collecting boxes should remain stationary and must not coerce passers-by or show intimidating behaviour.

C: Collections have to be made in sealed boxes - usually available from the benefiting charity - unless specifically exempted (for instance during a street procession).

D: All collectors must be aged 16 or over and be acting voluntarily.

After the collection you may be asked to complete a form giving the Council information including the total amount collected, who counted it, and a list of all the collectors etc.

LOTTERIES

A lottery is any game of chance in which tickets are sold enabling the holder to possibly qualify for a prize or money. This could include raffles, sweepstakes, tombolas, etc. When you introduce an element of skill such as in 'Spot the Ball' or 'Guess the weight of the cake' it then becomes a competition and is not subject to such rigorous regulations. In simple terms there are three types of lotteries that an event organiser might be interested in. There is the private lottery where those taking part are members or guests. There is the small lottery which is run as incidental to the main event such as at fetes, bazaars, craft sales, etc. And there is the social lottery which is unrestricted by membership. There are others, particularly those covered by registration with the Gaming Board, but these are unlikely to be considered by committees of small and medium scale one-off shows.

PRIVATE LOTTERIES

The regulations that cover games of chance are included in the Lotteries and Amusements Act, 1976. There are a few exemptions and it is these, fortunately, that are the most useful. Raffles are the most usual form of lottery and are perfectly legal without registration providing the sale of tickets, draw and allocation of prizes all happens during the course of the event, (i.e. a private lottery). There is no limit to the size of the lottery or on the price of the tickets. A good example is where cloakroom tickets are given out when people leave their coats prior to a Dinner Dance; after the coffee a draw takes place and bottles of wine, chocolates etc. are collected by the winners. Another exemption is serial-numbered programmes; these can be printed with individual numbers and again prizes offered for selected numbers before the end of the event. A private lottery must not be advertised outside the premises of the society or club.

SMALL LOTTERIES

Many events will include small lotteries such as 'Mark the spot where the Treasure is' or a tombola and it is important to note the rules that are attached to this type of activity.

As stated above, the lottery must not provide the main attraction and the whole activity must take place on the premises or site of your event and be concluded by the time everyone has left. As in private lotteries there is no restriction on the size of the lottery or the price of tickets but you cannot offer cash prizes, and the prizes that are offered should not exceed more than £50 in total; which is quite limiting when you think of the accumulative price of bottles on a bottle stall. Finally, there should be no element of private gain in holding either the lottery or the main event.

SOCIAL LOTTERIES

For a more effective lottery involving the sale of tickets over a period of time (social lotteries) you will need to go through the process of registration with the Local Authority (usually through the Administration Department). This is really only cost effective if your group is to hold regular lotteries. It currently (1992) costs £35 for initial registration, which covers you until

KEY POINTS

1. Ensure that public safety is not jeopardised and that you are not infringing people's basic rights

2. If you are selling alcohol you will need a Liquor Licence

3. If you are holding an event where singing or dancing is the main attraction you will require a Public Entertainment Licence

4. Check that your raffle or lottery is exempt from the terms of the Lotteries Act or register with the local authority

5. Consider competitions in favour of lotteries

6. Check before you apply for a licence that your show is not likely to run into problems. You will have to pay the application fee whether or not the licence is granted

7. Enquire about your council's attitude to Sunday trading

8. Remember that the Health and Safety at Work Act covers ALL activities that take place in the public domain

9. Make yourself aware of any local bye-laws that may affect you

10. Don't forget to register well in advance if you plan to have a collection on public property

11. If you are using a commercial fair make sure that every ride has it's 'MOT' and that you obtain a Safety Certificate for the whole fairground

12. Be aware of the dangers of inflatable castles

the next 1st January when a renewal fee of £17.50 is payable. Unless you apply for cancellation a renewal fee is due every New Year. The registration allows you to hold a lottery as follows:

REQUIREMENTS FOR RUNNING A LOTTERY

A: Registration is only possible if you are already an established group and fundraising for charitable purposes.

B: If the Authority agrees to registration a certificate will be granted, but you have the right to appeal if your group is not successful.

C: Proceeds must not exceed £10,000 and prizes may only be offered up to £2,000 in amount or value. If you exceed these limits your lottery must also be registered with the Gaming Board.

D: Expenses may be appropriated providing they are accurate and not more than 25% of the proceeds.

E: You may hold up to 52 lotteries in a year.

F: You must only sell tickets to people of 16 or over.

G: Each ticket or chance should be sold at a price of £1.00 or under; every ticket should be the same and show the cost on the ticket itself.

H: Each prize should be offered against one ticket only.

I: Afterwards, the promoter must make a return to the Local Authority on the form provided, within three months of the date when the lottery was held.

There are, of course, other more specific rules but these are the regulations germane to the operation of any lottery. If you are seriously considering registration there is a helpful leaflet on the Lotteries and Amusements Act - Cat No. B.L.5 from Shaw & Sons Ltd. (address at the back of the book) but it should be available from any Local Authority.

If you are concerned or worried about any exemption or procedure involving raffles or lotteries a quick call to the Council should clarify things.

COMPETITIONS

Lotteries seem to be the more popular form of additional entertainment at many events. But when you consider the regulations and restrictions that surround them it is surprising that competitions have not overtaken lotteries in the popularity stakes. Sorry! No pun intended.

Competitions include any activity where the outcome of the event is decided by skill or judgement of the player. Even where there is a mixture of skill and luck this is still classified as a competition. A draw to win a car is a typical example. The draw alone would not be legal since the prize is worth more than the £2,000 limit. But introduce a tie-break sentence for the two potential winners pulled out of the hat, and you now have a perfectly legal competition.

There are no restrictions on the amount of money taken or any limit on the value of the prizes. Indeed you at liberty to offer cash prizes. So my advice is to forget lotteries; go for competitions every time.

PUBLIC AREAS, FOOTPATHS AND RIVERS

Public areas and footpaths are often covered by local bye-laws and if there are conditions covering these they will be pointed out in the contract if you are hiring a council owned venue.

The sort of bye-laws that may affect you are whether you are allowed to fence off a footpath or indeed an entire public area (usually provision is made in the bye-law for a prescribed number of days closure per year) or you may be advised that no event can be held between certain hours or even that you have to leave the children's playground free for public use.

Concessionary cafes or shops can also cause problems, sometimes restricting the use of further caterers or food vans. Most Recreation Departments will cover these points for you but you do need to be aware of what might be the complaint when the Park Cafe manager starts shouting at you and waving his arms about in fury.

If you plan to use the stream or river at the bottom of your site for entertainment e.g. a raft race or boat procession, it may be that you will need permission from the local River or Waterways Authority. If the water is navigable you will certainly have to speak to them before you plan anything. Your local council can advise you where to go for help as they will be in constant communication with the correct organisation and will know the potential problems.

SUNDAY TRADING LAWS

Whether you feel that the Sunday Trading laws in this country are archaic and anachronistic or a necessary protection for peace one day a week, the reality is that they can cause a great many problems for Sunday fetes, fairs and Car Boot Sales in certain parts of the country. There are no hard and fast rules and every Local Authority has its own way of dealing with the law as stated in the Shops Act 1950 which allows sale of only limited items - mainly restricted to food, flowers and tourist guides etc. - on a Sunday. Some councils have a policy of ignoring all sales unless they are the subject of complaints, some prosecute every contravention and some seem to turn a blind eye to all Sunday trading.

I have often run events on a Sunday where there have been stalls and sales pitches but on the whole this was only secondary to the main feature and did not contribute greatly to the show. Some authorities will overlook this breach of the law but others will object at any stall selling goods that are not exempt. One of my events, however, was largely made up of stalls and was overrun by angry organisers of a Car Boot Sale that was to have happened on the same day in another area of the city but had been prevented by application of the Act. They understandably felt singled out and that they had been treated unfairly. The public and stall holders suffered harassment and jeers and the whole event became unpleasant and rather frightening; indeed the Police had to be called. I even had one 'Car Booter' follow me around Norwich, shouting and threatening me whenever I left the office during the next week.

For some reason tempers run high on the subject of Sunday trading, so if you know that you have an event that is based around selling things, you may be wise to arrange it for any day other than a Sunday. There is no point being provocative and you could just find yourselves with a court case on your hands.

HEALTH AND SAFETY AT WORK

The Health and Safety at Work Act is not only concerned with people in a formal place of work engaged in paid work for a registered company or individual. It is a 'catch all' law that is intended to protect everybody and anybody who is working with the public, paid or voluntarily. It is also particularly concerned with protecting third parties, for example the innocent passer-by who has something fall on his head from above. If an accident occurs as a result of activities taking place because of your event the investigating authority will be looking for someone on whom to pin the blame and prosecute. That will almost certainly be the organising group of the event.

Any activity that involves scaffolding or building work of any kind will be classified as 'construction' and the laws surrounding this work are very stringent. If you are using scaffolding or towers, even to make a small grandstand for instance, you would be well advised to have it erected professionally; thus taking the onus off yourselves.

Any group organising any event other than a few stalls or teas and games should study a very readable and clear government publication called 'Essentials of Health and Safety at Work'. All types of work and activity are covered and it gives very practical and easy-to-use guidelines on avoiding hazards and what to do in emergencies. It is a sobering thought that every year over 500 people lose their lives whilst engaged in work activities and thousands more are injured or suffer work-induced illness.

FAIRGROUNDS AND SAFETY CERTIFICATES

Most fairgrounds are owned by professional showmen. You can sometimes book individual rides but more usually you employ the whole works - rides, stalls, candyfloss pitches, everything. You can let them come onto the site free of charge as an added attraction but most showmen will think it worth their while to pay £200 - £300 for the pitch. Showmen can be intimidating if you have never worked with them before and you need to be clear what it is that you require from them and what they expect from you and what your rights are.

Most showmen prefer to work the sites that they are familiar with and in the main they are likely to turn up as planned if they are not going to somewhere new, especially if they have paid a pitch fee in advance, but you cannot always rely on them. This may seem unfair to those fairground operators who always behave honourably, but this is my opinion after many years working with showmen.

If the event is organised by you or your club and a fair is present at your invitation it is your responsibility to check the safety of the site. It will be your insurance which has to pay up if there is an accident. Every ride has an annual inspection, rather like an MOT, and is given a certificate if it is safe. You have a right to see all the certificates. You will also have to ensure that the site is safe after the fair is set up. You will need to arrange for an inspector who is a member of the National Association for Leisure Industry Certificates to visit the site a few hours before it opens to the public. You can ask for a list of qualified inspectors from your local Health and Safety Office or your local council may well employ a qualified engineer themselves; most of the time this is not a problem but in East Anglia, uniquely, they are few and far between so you will need to book somebody well in advance if your event is in this area. This is arranged at the showmen's expense and they know that they will have to pay the electrician before they can be issued with a Safety Certificate.

You can give the area the once-over before the inspector comes so that you can point out anything that worries you. The sort of things that you should be looking for are whether the gangways are clear and wide enough to get the emergency services through if needed. Are all the cables heavy duty and weather proof? If they cross gangways they need to be flown above seven feet or dug into the ground so that they cannot be tripped over. Do the rides look well maintained or are safety rails missing or moving parts unprotected?

If you are unhappy with any aspect of your fair or the behaviour of the showmen running it you can complain to the Showman's Guild of Great Britain - your local section secretary will be listed in the telephone directory.

INFLATABLE CASTLES

At present there are no laws governing bouncy castles but I feel it will not be long before this is looked at. There have been some truly appalling accidents in recent years - over 4,000 children are injured annually in the UK - through negligence and thoughtless use; absolutely anybody can buy a castle and set themselves up as a hire company with no training or registration. Inflatable castles or rides should be tied down with guy-ropes, as in even the lightest of breezes they can take off and scatter children onto the ground resulting in injury or at the very least cause them to be very frightened and use should be cancelled completely in rain due to the slippery surfaces. One adult should always be present within the castle to help children if they panic or are jumped on. Times restricted to certain age groups and limiting children on the castle at any one time to a safe number can all help keep accidents to a minimum, but the children still need supervision. If there seems to be any problem at all with the blower or the possibility of a puncture, the castle should be cleared until it is certain that the castle is fully inflated and likely to stay that way.

You may also be aware of the new 'Bar Jump' or 'Sticky Castles' that are now available. These have been very popular in Australia and look like a regular castle except that the flat back to the rear of the inside is covered in very strong velcro. The 'bouncers' wear velcro suits and after working up their bouncing to a good height they then throw themselves at the sticky wall and stick: like flies in a spiders web! It is great fun and reasonably safe as long as no more than two jumpers are taking part at a time. Restrict times to about 5 minutes each. In my experience people, especially adults, will be off long before the time is up. It is one of the most exhausting activities that I have ever tried.

Whilst there are no statutory regulations as yet the Health and Safety Executive have very recently issued detailed safety guidelines. HSE Guidance Note PM76 is available from HMSO stockists.

17 ON SITE

So now you have got to the day itself. You will feel a mixture of excitement and apprehension rather like stage fright. And you deserve a pat on the back for having come this far; many lesser mortals fall by the wayside under the weight of regulations, unhelpful suppliers or just when the full enormity of what they are taking on dawns on them. But you are not through the woods yet.

If your event is small or able to be run with just the committee members on the day then, hopefully, you will all have been present during the planning and know what your separate responsibilities are. However for larger shows you will now be facing a line of volunteers and it is your job to make sure that everyone knows what their job is, what the emergency procedures are, where the nearest telephone is, where the first aid is positioned, where the fire exits are if you are indoors and what you will be doing in case they get stuck and need to find you.

If you need to keep in contact by radio, now is the time to hand them out and make sure that they will be used properly. Remember to remind operators where the chargers will be kept.

You do not need to wear uniforms, of course, unless you are official stewards in a show-ring in which case it is traditional to wear a dark suit and a bowler hat (even the women!). However it helps for you, at least, to wear something distinctive - a brightly coloured tracksuit is fine but in my experience arm bands cannot be seen and fall off after a while anyway.

FINAL INSTRUCTIONS AND CHECKS

I find it helpful to issue everyone with a site plan, which includes the Police emergency number and a running list, and just spend five minutes talking it through with them. Arrive having worked out what needs to be done beforehand and offer jobs around rather than dole them out. Helpers tend to volunteer for the jobs for which they are most able or like best so are less likely to get bored and wander off.

However many times you have checked things before, make a final check over the whole site or building about 15 minutes before you open. You will be surprised how many things have been moved or lost at the last minute.

Make sure that everyone knows where your 'base' is. If your event covers a large site and you are not in touch using radios ensure that your Public Address system covers all the important parts of the show-ground. If you have neither radios or a PA system at an event such as an orienteering day, make an arrangement where you agree to be at a certain spot every hour or half hour. Don't forget to synchronise watches!

RUNNING ORDERS

You will need to have worked out a running order well before the show, probably down to the minute. Pack things together tightly and have plenty going on at once. Events are best when there is a sense of urgency about the day. They seem really tedious when you have to wait 15 minutes between each item.

It is strange but when performers are good and a show is going well everything seems to speed up. (The exception to this rule is pantomime, the performers often get so carried away that several minutes can be added in the form of off-the-cuff responses to the audience). The adrenaline is high and even animals move faster so you can suddenly be left with a long gap between acts. Make sure that you programme in lunch and tea breaks to soak up the gaps or catch up with yourselves if you are running late. (It is better to run late than early). The public can spend the time looking at the stands or getting something to eat as long as they expect a pause but they won't stay for long if everything starts to drag.

Most people will not stay at any event for longer than about two or three hours, families with small children will frequently

KEY POINTS

1 Enjoy the day and try to have everything precisely planned before you arrive.

2 Inform all your helpers of the running order, all the tasks and clearing up jobs before you start. Allow them to choose what they will be doing.

3 Ensure everyone knows where the nearest telephone and first aid kit is. Give out emergency numbers if necessary.

4 Check everything 15 minutes before you open.

5 Keep your show tightly packed with activities and remember to plan meal breaks where appropriate.

6 Keep the public informed of changes to the advertised programme.

7 After the entrance money has been collected for an indoor show remove cash to a safe area.

8 Use a clip board.

9 Remember to bring an 'emergencies box'.

stay less, so if you plan a show to be open for four or five hours you will catch nearly everyone who wants to come and they will be left feeling they would like a little more and might well come again another time.

If your event is really a competition that is open to the public such as a Horticultural Show or Cat Show ensure that all the serious technical stuff is done in the morning and get the bulk of the competition out of the way by lunch time. Keep the 'Best in Show' for the last class of the day, and whilst the jury are out deciding you could give the audience something rather more lighthearted to enjoy such as a demonstration and then end with a parade or procession if appropriate.

At an indoor event your volunteers will probably be acting as ushers/usherettes. Remember that people will want somewhere to leave coats if there is no room by their seats or if it is a party;

▶▶ BILL'S PROGRESS

Bill didn't sleep very well but as he drives to Brick Close estate he is too excited to think about how tired he is. In the back of his van he has a box full of equipment that he thinks might be needed during the course of the event. He has a folder of volunteers' instructions and site plans, a megaphone that he scrounged off someone at work, the film projector and the RSPCA exhibition already mounted on boards protected by two large portfolios. Bill was thrilled with the finished result when he collected it from the office yesterday. Two colleagues had been working on it for over a month and they had produced a really top-class, eye-catching and informative exhibition.

He had taken the film itself over to Olivia Knight on Wednesday evening so she could familiarize herself with the reel-changes and check the running times.

He is looking forward to meeting Arthur Pint on site to go over the final details before the other volunteers arrive. He glances out of the window and sees with satisfaction and not a little relief that the sun is shining brightly and it looks set to be a warm, dry day.

Bill knows that all is in hand and allows himself a nervous smile of anticipation as he swings into the playground gate and sees his friend run towards the car...

they might feel happier about leaving their belongings if you have a cloakroom attendant. As in the outdoor events, it helps if all 'staff' are dressed in a similar way but as the whole show is much more intimate badges might be adequate. Decide where your base will be - preferably a private room where you can lock away the entrance money when the show starts - and ensure that all your helpers know where you will be.

HANDY HINTS

Use a clip-board. It may seem stereotypical to be seen running around with a clip-board under your arm but it is the only way I know of keeping all your information together and instantly accessible without getting lost or blowing away. Any extra piece of information that anyone gives you can be quickly secured and you have a continuous reminder of important items in your hand. If you can find one that has a fold over or fold down waterproof cover, all the better, some even have little pockets to put small items in which can be very useful and I always attach a pencil with a piece of string so that I never have to waste time looking for one.

Keep an 'emergencies-box' in your car or office adjusted to the size and style of event. This could contain 6-10 sheets of white A2 stiff card; permanent, thick felt pens of varying colours and a stencil if you lack confidence as to your sign-writing prowess; two balls of string - one thick, one thin, a pair of very serviceable scissors; Sellotape, thick insulating tape or gaffer-tape if you can find it or afford it; a heavy-duty staple gun; a tape measure; a basic tool kit; a first aid kit; a small portable fire extinguisher and a bottle of drink and packet of biscuits or, if you are very efficient, some sandwiches. If your event is outside you could add a hand held megaphone and even a change of clothes and a sun-hat. I once was helping to put up a marquee on the river bank when the man hauling up a guy rope opposite me saw his wife going down the tow-path the wrong way and ran to head her off whilst letting go of the rope. The ridge pole fell down and the weight of canvas knocked me into the river. I spent the whole of the rest of the event in a borrowed track suit, three times too big, in baking sunshine!

With the above you should be able to design notices at the drop of a hat, make running repairs, put out minor fires, aid the injured, shout instructions, keep yourself in good working order and keep the sun off your head if you know it affects you. Eight hours outside without respite can be very demanding.

18 ASSUMING THE WORST (OR PLAN 'B')

REASONS FOR LAST MINUTE CHANGES

In this country the major reason for outdoor events being cancelled or changes made to the advertised schedule has to be because of the weather. Great Britain is known for its rain, although in past years I have known of sports events postponed not due to rain but because the pitch or courts have dried and cracked up. But in general it is the rain or cold that defeats us and all events organisers scan the sky suspiciously on the morning of The Day.

Do not think that because your event may be indoors that you are immune. Oh no! The public are just as picky about coming out of their nice warm homes on a snowy evening to travel to the Village Hall or Community Centre to see the 'am-dram' Panto.

You must build potential losses due to cloudbursts or July hail into your pricing structure; see Chapter 6 in the section on Marketing for figures to work to. And you can do a great deal to allow for problems by making contingency plans.

Other unforeseen problems can include accidents on the main route to your venue, burst pipes (both indoors and out), and contractors starting work the day before your show in the middle of the site. Equipment or Acts can be delayed or just simply not turn up, performers suddenly take to their beds or, as happened to me on one ill-fated day, the sheep due to take part in the sheep dog demonstration escaped and refused to be caught for over an hour, even by the champion sheep dog who had been brought for the purpose. This was the same show - indeed the same performer - whose performing ducks, being so used to the act, did everything before they were asked to with such bored and resigned looks that the very good humoured audience ended up shouting the orders!

All the above have happened to one of my shows at one time or another, sometimes more than once but I have never had to cancel. We have moved most of an event into a marquee and held a horse show in pouring rain, a jazz night took place in a tent that nearly took off with the force of the wind and the Police once had to close the roads half an hour earlier than advertised due to holiday traffic chaos, leaving people stranded around the city (my family included, who I don't think ever believed that I could organise anything at all after that little fiasco). The Lions Club once had such a successful charity collection - over £7,000 in loose change - that we nearly broke the back axle of the collection van, and the smallest boy at the top of a sea scout pyramid lighting a beacon to mark the anniversary of the Armada singed his eyebrows off and had to have minor emergency treatment.

You just cannot foretell these kind of problems but if they occur - and something surprising always does - you will have to make a swift decision and act on it immediately. The worst that can happen is that you cannot be there on the day and that is when it is vital that all your plans, running orders and contacts are on paper for someone else to be able to use. The second worse is that you are there but fail to make a decision; someone else will and may make the wrong one: you will still be blamed - and quite rightly.

LETTING THE PUBLIC KNOW

The easiest way of letting the public know that there is a change is to advertise it in advance and there are occasions when this is possible, for instance if a performer pulls out of the show a couple of weeks before the date or you have to change a venue because the auditorium suffered a serious fire. You can only do this, of course, if the problem has manifested itself far enough in advance.

The weather, whilst being a more immediate problem can be catered for in the form of 'In the Village Hall if wet', everyone now knows that if it looks like rain the event will still take place but in an alternative venue. A car boot sale or Mammoth Fair is more of a challenge but you can usually rely on hardy members of the public and the stalwart buyers and sellers to come despite the rain even if the event is not as popular as you had hoped.

There are the odd occasions when you really will have to cancel everything at short notice or move everybody a mile down the road or perhaps postpone things for an hour or two and the very best way of getting the public in the picture is to broadcast the changes on local radio. Telephone your local radio station and explain the problem and they will almost certainly be glad to assist. Once the word is out you can then back up the news with handwritten posters (make sure that you have pens and paper in your on-the-day-kit) or by announcing the new plans or reasons for the delay over a loudspeaker if possible.

• • • • • • • • • • •

KEY POINTS

❶ Advertise all advance changes as soon as you know them

❷ Try to have considered potential problems, especially the weather and decide on alternative arrangements with your committee so all you have to do on the day is switch to Plan B

❸ Never leave the public without information

❹ Use local radio to help broadcast the changes

❺ Make posters and use loud hailers to give information

❻ Don't panic and be decisive

Above all try not to keep a crowd hanging about without any explanation; people are understanding and although they may be disappointed or annoyed they can at least make an informed decision to stay or leave as long as they know the problem.

To go back to my introduction, what ever happens don't panic and you will be amazed at how little is noticed even when you think the circumstances are dire.

▶▶ BILL'S PROGRESS

As he turns into the playground at 6.30am Bill sees his friend Arthur Pint run over to the car.

"Daphne Furry has just rung to say that her son has been taken to hospital with suspected appendicitis. She can't be here to judge the show". Arthur's usual calm and slightly cynical attitude is conspicuous by its absence.

Bill's heart sinks. He looks at his watch and decides that it will be at least another hour before he can ring Rufus Byte from Calamity Kennels to suggest another judge.

"We've got half an hour before the volunteers arrive", says Bill. " Lets open up the Centre and get the exhibition up as planned and when the others are all here you can go back to the pub and ring Rufus".

They start to walk over to the Community Centre. Bill has a sudden thought, "why did Mrs Furry ring you and not Rufus?" he asks Arthur. "It seems he forgot to tell her his 'phone number when he booked her." said Arthur ruefully, "he saw her at some meeting, made the arrangement and she wasn't even sure of the name of his kennels."

As they are putting up the exhibition boards Bill thinks of the empty space in his checklist and knows that he can't blame Rufus. He should have insisted on a follow up letter; or he should have done it himself. Still he must get his other helpers organised and they are now starting to arrive. Bill briefs Herb about Arthur's trade stalls and asks him to stand in if necessary.

At 7.15am Arthur walks round to the pub to make his telephone call. He glances back to see Bill making sure that everyone knows what is expected of them. By now they all are aware of the problem that they might have but Bill says not to worry until they have to.

By ten minutes to nine the Girl Guides have arrived and are setting out the tea tent (the marquee went up the night before) the chairs have been collected from the church hall and the children are arriving at the school to prepare for the parade. The Red Cross representatives have made a base in the small meeting room of the Community Centre and still Arthur is not back from the pub. Bill decides to wait ten more minutes before going to find him.

Just then Arthur arrives, puffing like an express train, his face wreathed in smiles. "Its OK" he tells anyone who wants to hear. "Rufus gave me the name of another judge". He stops to catch his breath. "I rang him; he'll be here at ten and Molly will collect him from the station".

So Bill feels himself come back from certain oblivion! He lets the competitors know that the show may be a few minutes late in starting and when Rufus arrives a quarter of an hour later he thanks him for his quick thinking and fills him in as to the adjustment in their schedule. Rufus makes an announcement at the start of the Dog Show but by the end of the third class they have caught up anyway so by the time most of the public arrive at midday everything is back on course again.

19 SAFETY, SECURITY, CHILDREN AND DISABLED PEOPLE

It may seem strange to lump all four of the above subjects together and I accept that needs, especially, for people who have to use wheelchairs, are visually handicapped or deaf are very different from those of children or indeed their carers. However, it is a fact of life that all four are sometimes forgotten or at least only given cursory consideration during the excitement and enthusiasm of setting up an event.

SAFETY

Your prime responsibility to the general public, and indeed your fellow workers, is not to give them a good time or even to make a good profit. It is to keep them as safe as is reasonably possible, while doing so. Of course, people have a responsibility not to put themselves in danger but they also have a right to assume that if they enter a marquee that it will not fall down or that the lighting rig hung above their heads is strong enough to support the twenty lights that you have suspended on it.

Most of the equipment you use will be simple enough for anyone to check for safety but, apart from the inspections required by law covered in Chapters 7 & 16, you would be advised to get an electrician to look over all temporary electrical fittings.

Ensure that there are no piles of rubbish casually lying about waiting for a lighted cigarette-end, and watch the positioning of electric tea urns. I have heard of two accidents caused by someone walking into the flex and spilling gallons of boiling water over the tea-ladies.

Caterers coming to your event are doing a job of work and are covered by the Health and Safety at Work Act (as you are; see Chapter 16), they must comply with the guidelines laid down and you should be able to co-operate as much as possible.

Other obvious problems to look out for are possible tripping hazards, especially cables across walkways, loose guy ropes and tent pegs. Routes for cars should, where possible, be sited separately from paths for pedestrians, and shade provided at a show where there are animals present.

Ensure that you go for 100% safety if your event is near water or on the sea-shore: a tragedy is all too easy. A word with the Police to establish a procedure in the event of an accident is a very worthwhile task and could save someone's life. Make sure that all the helpers know what to do as well as yourself.

SECURITY

You can read more on this subject in Chapter 13 but I suggest that whenever money is carried around it should be accompanied by two people and, where large amounts of cash are expected, they should be removed to a place of safety regularly.

On the whole potential criminals at an event are interested in very little other than money, alcohol and cigarettes. Alcohol and cigarettes should only be sold from a restricted area or a designated bar and money should be kept on site for as short a time as possible and even then kept in a place where there is no public access.

Occasionally prizes or cups might prove attractive to the opportunist thief and it is probably sensible to keep them out of sight.

One other security problem is people trying to enter your showground or building without paying. This is almost impossible to control on a large outdoor event site but with limited entrances, reasonably substantial fencing and a couple of large people making regular patrols to repair any gaps you should be

KEY POINTS

1. You have a responsibility to keep everyone involved with your event safe at all times

2. Watch for fire hazards, tripping hazards and make sure that cars are kept away from pedestrian areas

3. Check the whole area before it opens and ensure that all electrical equipment is inspected by a qualified electrician

4. Remove cash to a secure place regularly

5. Ensure that alcohol and cigarettes are sold from restricted areas and that after an event they are removed as quickly as possible

6. Keep prizes out of sight

7. Be aware of possible weaknesses in your security fencing for outside events and use security people on tent exits if necessary

8. Try not to use pass-out tickets as they are open to abuse

9. Give due consideration to children's needs and think about the advantages that a creche can bring

10. Remember the needs of all disabled peopled not just those with obvious difficulties. Ask for help from an experienced organisation if necessary

Provide a cordial
atmosphere at any
event where you
expect families.

able to keep illegal entries to a minimum. For people wanting to go off the site and return later you will need to give pass-outs; the simplest workable method is to rubber-stamp their hands. A stamped hand is difficult to pass to someone over the fence but ticket pass-outs are wide open to abuse. Because of the closed nature of a building you should have little difficulty with security but a tent may present more of a challenge. You will have to have several exits in a tent for emergencies but, unlike a building, you will not be able to keep them shut with crash bars. To be absolutely certain you catch everyone at the official entrance you will have to put a 'bouncer' on each exit, at least until the show is well under way.

CHILDREN

You should think about providing a cordial atmosphere at any event where you expect families or even unaccompanied older children. We have an unfortunate reputation in this country for not providing enough facilities to enable the 'family outing' to be a pleasurable affair but perhaps with a little thought we can begin to undo this poor opinion. At the lower end of the age group a small tent or caravan designated as a 'Mother and Baby' room is an unusual but welcome addition at an outdoor event. A low chair for nursing in private and a trestle table for baby-changing with a covered bin nearby for rubbish is all that is needed. A soft drinks bar for under 18s to purchase their own refreshments means that the main bar is less crowded and allows children a little independence.

At a fairground it can be helpful if an area is sectioned off for little ones only to play. This can include a ball pond, bouncy castle (see Chapter 16 for safety), and small roundabouts.

For some events it may be worth considering opening a short term creche (less than two hours or you will have to register with your Local Authority). A Christmas Craft Fair might be all the better for giving parents the opportunity to browse quietly around the stands for a precious hour knowing that their toddlers and babies were being looked after by responsible carers. It is most important to find qualified creche leaders and assistants and you can talk to your local social services department to get advice on setting up a creche or you can hire a mobile care unit (see address at the back of the book). There is a useful publication available through any HMSO bookshop which details part of the Children

Act 1989 called 'Guidance Regulations Vol II. Family Support and Day Care Provision for Young Children'. You should take particular note of the ratio of children per carer which will vary depending on the age of the children.

Remember, also, to fix a point for lost children. The secretary's tent or front-of-house manager's office are good choices as they will usually have access to a public address system.

DISABLED PEOPLE

Many disabled people, who would otherwise love a day out in the open air or a visit to a Christmas Carol Concert in the local church, feel that the effort and worry of being away from home is not worth the nevertheless undoubted pleasure of the event. The thought of tripping up unfamiliar steps in the car park at night, scraping knuckles while trying to negotiate a narrow doorway in a wheelchair or simply being unable to hear properly is sometimes just too daunting and sadly many of the population who could most benefit from a good time feel that most amateur (and a good many professional) events are not for them.

The most obvious facility to provide is a loo suitable for someone in a wheelchair or who has to use a walking frame (see Chapter 9 for where to obtain these). Remember to site these on reasonably firm ground as it can be very difficult trying to push a chair over mud, gravel or spongy grass. Make sure that the entrance to the site is wide enough for a chair or for someone with seeing difficulties to have a guide walk beside them - about 1 metre should do. If your event is at night make sure that all steps and car parks are illuminated - this makes sense for able bodied people also - or provide a guide with a torch.

For seated shows it is not enough to remove a seat for a wheelchair; you must also ensure that the space is level and has enough leg room. People do not appreciate falling over hard footplates in the dark and for the owner of the chair it can be very painful. It makes sense to situate people with difficulties near an exit for their convenience and to help clear the auditorium quickly in an emergency but do make sure that they will be able to see the performance adequately.

Anybody who is hard of hearing and wears a hearing aid will tell you how effective a hearing loop system is in a theatre. It can make all the difference to an evening's entertainment and is well worth enquiring about when you hire a building.

And as a last word on the subject, do not think that it is only those of us who are mentally 'normal' who can enjoy events. During a week's showing of 'Colourscape' - an extraordinary sculptural experience where participants were encouraged to wear matching cloaks and wander through six foot high brightly coloured pods - I watched a severely mentally and physically handicapped boy crawl his way through the sculpture time and time again, pausing occasionally to enjoy the whirling colours and warmth, and laughing and chuckling with pure joy at the wonderful sensation of freedom that it gave him. It was most revealing when I realised that he was getting more out of the show than any other person there.

20 AFTERWARDS

How you cope with winding your event up can be almost as important as getting it off the ground. If you are planning another show on the same lines next year your attitude at the end of this year can make a big difference to the help and services that you can expect subsequently.

The end of an event can bring satisfaction, realization of a job well done and a sense of achievement. This is how one imagines it should feel but often these positive emotions are delayed and overcome by weariness, a feeling of anti-climax and occasionally disappointment if things have not gone according to plan.

Tempers can be frayed towards the end of the day and sometimes the organiser feels let down by fellow helpers who drift away leaving him/her to deal with the final arrangements. It is important to have invited takers for clearing up jobs before the event starts so that volunteers know the extent of their duties or have an opportunity to warn you that they can only stay until an appointed hour.

Don't worry if you feel depressed when it is all over, the elation will soon be there, especially after a good night's sleep. After all, you have been running on extra adrenaline and under tremendous stress all through the show and probably several days before; your body is worn out. Because of these down feelings that you can experience it is important to hold a de-briefing session - I dislike calling these post-mortems - where you will of course discuss your final tasks but you should also allow yourselves time to go through the good and the bad points, to have a laugh and commiserate

KEY POINTS

1. Try not to be disappointed if you feel that the end of the day is an anti-climax. Ensure that you get together with your fellow organisers and discuss all the highs as well as the lows

2. Ensure that you have arranged who will tackle individual clearing up jobs before the day gets under way

3. Do the jobs that must be done right away but if the hour is late make sure that everything else is secure and leave it until tomorrow

4. Be aware of the risks of vandalism

5. Be sure to complete your accounts properly

6. Be sure to thank all volunteers and contributors

7. If you have been fundraising make sure that you make the most of the presentation, you may want to use it as a means to thank all who helped

if necessary, give praise where it is due and be gracious enough to accept a few pats on the back; you will have deserved them.

CLEARING UP

Leaving a site or venue clean always takes longer than you think and if you have a large show to tidy up after it is wise to make arrangements to leave things secure on site, if possible, so that you can finish off the next day.

Certain jobs should be done as soon as possible. Removing money to a more secure place, even before it has been counted is vital after a large outdoor event. All food waste and wrappers should be collected and disposed of either to the local tip or in a skip hired for the purpose. Lavatories should be cleaned or at the very least locked until they can be dealt with hygienically, and, unless you are very sure of the weather, tents and marquees should be taken down. PA systems, sound mixing desks, loud-speaker towers, and lighting rigs should all be disconnected and, if not removed immediately, made secure; there is a very real risk of overnight vandalism. All electrical supplies and generators should also be disconnected and made safe.

It is helpful if you can find out when the next booking is due, if you have hired a hall, and whether a cleaner will be coming in. You may be expected to sweep up yourselves and you will not want to be left having to do all the dirty work on your own.

If your event is outside you will need to a organise a thorough check on foot to ensure that there are no fence posts, tents pegs, piles of rubbish or other hazards left on the site. I once found an abandoned car in a field that we had to have towed away at our expense and more than once I have had to beg a favour from a local diver to pull all manner of things out of the river. Why do people bring supermarket trolleys to outdoor events and how do they get them there?

Your main problem will be litter but if you read Chapter 9 you should be well prepared.

FINAL BUDGETS AND
THE PRESENTATION TO CHARITY

At your final meeting you should go through the accounts and complete your actuals. If you have been fundraising you will have to agree, if you have not already made a decision, what part of the proceeds will be passed over. The treasurer can draw a cheque -

the Bank will be happy to prepare a giant-sized copy if you warn them in advance - so that you can present your donation at a pre-arranged reception having made sure that the press and rest of the media will be there. You should milk the publicity as much as you can, it will please the charity and any sponsors as well as giving your group credibility for future endeavours.

If you have opened a Bank account peculiar to this show, keep it open for another month just in case other expenses filter through and then close it or, if you intend to run your event next year, ask your Bank manager if you can keep the account open but suspended until you need it again. You should then be able to benefit from free banking each year (see Chapter 12).

THANK YOU LETTERS AND STAYING IN TOUCH

Thank you letters are very welcome and really help to make people feel positively enthusiastic about assisting on future occasions. If you have used the skills of many people all from one club then individual letters will not be necessary. A single letter addressed to the senior member but expressing gratitude to all who gave their time is much appreciated.

For those who lent property and belongings, firstly ensure that they received their things back in good order and then thank them individually. Any damage or loss must be made good immediately.

Some organising groups may decide to help a specific organisation exclusively or for an allotted span of time. These groups or clubs may very well welcome a newsletter from their chosen charity or appreciate an invitation for one of their members to join the organising committee next time.

Sometimes a very labour intensive event has just so many individuals to thank that it can be worth inviting everyone who participated to the charity presentation, see above, or to a separate 'thank you' party. This is a lovely way to wind up months and months of work and ends the whole business on a really memorable note.

▶▶ BILL'S PROGRESS

As the last people leave the recreation ground and a straggle of children gather up their costumes Bill wanders over to his policeman friend. John is sitting on the grass beside the big German Shepherd dog who performed so well during the afternoon and looks up at Bill who has just come out of the Community Centre having thanked all his volunteers for their hard work.

"Went well", he smiles. "You should be really pleased, you got a good band of people to work with."

"Yup" says Bill, "I'll reckon I'll give it another go next year" he says over his shoulder as he walks over to collect the rubbish bins.

"Hang on", his friend shouts after him, "you've not finished clearing up this one yet!"

A couple of weeks later the team is back together again in 'the Bowl and Whistle'. The committee has decided to present a cheque for £300 to the RSPCA at a special launch that is planned for a new initiative. John Wright from the Red Tile Co. has donated £200 to be put on deposit as a pump primer for next year's show: there will be another Dog Day next year. And Bill has had many messages of thanks and congratulations. Daphne Furry's son is out of hospital and she has promised to be the judge next year.

But best of all are the three members from Brick Close estate who will be joining the committee for next year with a commitment to bring more entertainment and education to their own neck of the woods.

Bill has achieved his objectives. The exhibition created much discussion and is to be used on a regular basis around the region. The committee made enough money to cover their costs and had some spare to donate to the RSPCA. The community thoroughly enjoyed themselves; so much so that they definitely want the Dog Day to be repeated and are prepared to help with the preparations. It might take a little more than one show to have a really comfortable relationship with the Police but its going in the right direction.

And Bill?...Well Bill had some hairy moments but he worked through them, organised a great event, made some good friends and has gained a precious slice of confidence to help him with another show and his own work.

21 NEXT YEAR?

Some events are purely one-offs and some finish as a once only but many are planned as or evolve into annual shows.

If your show has gone well and the community really became part of it or you succeeded in raising several hundred pounds for your cause you will be wondering whether to repeat the work next year.

For a community event the surest way of guaranteeing success again is to hold an open meeting to discuss if the neighbourhood wish to repeat the exercise or if they prefer to wait a few years before having to commit themselves so thoroughly a second time.

Charity events may work well as an annual occurrence especially if they have been largely organised by a group or club which will be prepared to take them on year after year. Much of the hard work is in setting a show up for the first time and you will be able to draw on past experience and perhaps have some spare capacity to develop the event into a large-scale show over the next few years if that is what is wanted. Annual events work best if they are held around the same date each year and become an established part of the calendar.

Some events look, on the face of it, to be for one day only never to be held again, but with a little ingenuity even these can take on a new lease of life in further years. For instance a few years ago several events all around the country were held to mark the 400th anniversary of the vanquishing of the Spanish Armada. A once in a hundred years celebration we all thought, however many groups enjoyed running their events so much that annual Elizabethan shows have risen from the ashes giving a much appreciated platform for Early Dance Groups, Elizabethan instrument players and creative chefs.

PLANNING FOR NEXT YEAR

Having run a show once you will now know what you need as a basic structure for your event and you may well still have an organising committee in place.

Try not to be complacent about the time needed. Even if your event is not until late Summer you will still need to get moving early on if only to preclude the panic that you experienced last year! Have at least one meeting to consolidate your committee,

● ● ● ● ● ● ● ● ● ● ● ●

KEY POINTS

❶ Hold a public meeting or decide amongst yourselves if you wish the event to be repeated

❷ It can be a good idea to stick to the same date

❸ Use your imagination for continuing an event that might have looked like a 'once-only'

❹ Get the basic structure of a committee in place as soon as possible and do not be complacent about the preparation time. Get started early!

perhaps elect a new Chairman/woman, and get a feel for who would be interested in taking on specific duties. After the Christmas and New Year celebrations are behind you the real work should begin and you should now be following the timescales suggested in Chapter 11. If you plan a Christmas event it is hard to think about winter activities in the heat of the Summer but you will really need to start planning in May or June at the latest.

Whatever date your event is planned for allow at least six months to get things organised, and if your event is medium to large-scale or includes many elements you may have to start allow a lot longer.

22 CHARITABLE STATUS

Most groups and clubs that operate in a largely philanthropic way to assist the community or individuals by donating services, money, equipment or by providing education or recreation are registered charities in their own rights. And whilst it means that they have to have accounts open to inspection they benefit from all the grant and tax advantages afforded to trusts and charities.

If your event is an annual affair or your organising committee find yourselves involved in several fund raising activities each year it may be worth applying to the Charity Commission to register your group for charity status. Registration is not mandatory but 'Registration, once accepted, is conclusive proof that the organisation is entitled to the rate and tax advantages of a charity, but failure to register does not deprive the trust of its charitable character: it merely makes it harder to prove.'- Charles Arnold-Baker, 'Practical Law for Arts Administrators'. If you are fund raising for another charity each time you run an event you cannot create a new charity, but if you are running several events over a period of time to fundraise for a specific project (for instance a new Church Hall or fitting out a cruise boat to give handicapped children independent holidays) you may have a case to form a new charity. 'Fund raising is not a charitable purpose in itself. It has to be carried out in support of charitable purposes.' - 'Starting a Charity', Charity Commissioners for England and Wales.

The above quotation comes from a leaflet, No.CC21 which is freely available from the Charity Commission, St. Alban's House, 57/60 Haymarket, London SW1Y 4QX and gives a very good outline of how to start a new charity.

If you think that you might like to set up a charity, very briefly the procedure is as follows:

A. Prepare a draft governing document, if possible, based on an existing model.
B. Contact the Charity Commission and ask for a copy of the questionnaire which has to be completed before the Commissioners are prepared to consider your application.

KEY POINTS

❶ If you are conducting regular fundraising activities for a specific project you might consider registering for charitable status

❷ It is usually wiser to find an existing charity that already works in your chosen area and make donations directly to them but remember to ask permission first.

❸ If you are seriously deciding to opt for registration read some of the publications that are listed at the back of this book before you start

C. Complete the questionnaire and return it along with two copies of the draft governing document.

D. Further information may be required including clarification of your proposals and approval from the Inland Revenue.

For most one-off fund raising it is usually possible to find a charity which would be prepared to take on a particular project and, of course, you won't find many charities turning down the offer of more donations if you wish to fund raise in more general terms e.g. for the elderly (Age Concern) or animals (The Donkey Sanctuary).

However, you must remember that some charities' logos and names are a very commercial asset. The Charities Act, 1992 now makes provision for the prevention of any unauthorised fundraising. Before you hold an event to benefit any specified charity, however innocuous you think the event or your organisation is, you must obtain permission to use their name and give them a chance to suggest any provisos. There is unlikely to be much of a problem if the Round Table plan a jumble sale in aid of Oxfam but the World Wildlife Fund might take a pretty dim view if the local hunt were to hold a raffle in their name.

You will find some addresses at the back of the book along with some book titles that might be helpful if you wish to know more on this subject.

23 WORKING WITH ANIMALS

There are several types of shows that involve working with animals or birds. They can be divided into three groups; (a. those where the animals are demonstrating the way that they 'work' such as Sheep Dog Displays, Police Dog Handler Demonstrations, Ploughing Exhibitions or Carriage Driving Competitions; (b. those in which the animals are on show or judged for their form and beauty such as Agricultural Shows, Cat and Dog Shows, Horse shows, Bird of Prey Exhibitions or even perhaps, of a less formal nature, pens holding rabbits or goats for children to pet and stroke; and (c. where the animals and birds provide the actual entertainment having been trained to do tricks or clever acts that are not part of their usual behaviour or in their natural environment for instance within a Circus; these often include the use of 'exotics' which include tigers, seals, alligators etc. There are some shows where a combination of the above may be on offer.

There is one other way in which animals can become part of the attractions and this is where the event is held within their own environment, such as within a deer park or farm, but here the animals are incidental and probably not the direct responsibility of the event organiser, although safety of both visitors and animals will be a consideration.

PROFESSIONAL BODIES AND PERMISSIONS

There are certain shows and competitions which you will not be able to hold without approval or permission from the appropriate association. Bill Pincher

KEY POINTS

1. Remember to ensure that you have covered all the requirements made by the relevant professional body before you go ahead with any animal show

2. Consider having veterinary help on hand

3. Make sure that clean, fresh water is readily available and that you have provided all that is expected in the way of cages, pens etc.

4. Think hard before agreeing to using animal circus acts. You may have problems from the local Council and protesters

5. Make arrangements to have animal waste disposed of properly

6. Just occasionally you may be faced with unpleasant decisions involving injury or even death of an animal. Have a contingency plan ready

105

cannot, for instance hold an Exemption Dog Show without first obtaining a licence from the Kennel Club; if you wished to hold an Open Dog Show you would need to abide by the regulations set down and use approved judges. The same goes for all sorts of other pedigree competitions including Horse Shows, Cat Shows and Cage Bird Competitions.

If you are holding a children's Gymkhana in a local field with Apple Bobbing Races or Bareback Jumping classes the professional bodies are not going to give two hoots because you are not holding your event up to be a serious competition or indeed yourselves as experts in the judging of horseflesh. However you will be in trouble if you offer a Best of Breed Cup at your Heavy Horse Show if the judge is not on the approved list of the correct Association.

Clubs, associations and other relevant organisations can be of great assistance when working in a specialist field. They will often suggest the running order of the show for you, provide rosettes, prizes, programmes, numbers, cages and all sorts of other equipment sometimes free of charge. You will automatically have a listing in their news letters or magazines and have the most valuable 'word-of-mouth' advertising. See Chapter 5 and 6 for more ideas.

SPECIAL FACILITIES

The most obvious and vital facilities that you must make available if you are working with animals is water, food and shelter. Food will almost certainly be brought by the owners but they will expect fresh, clean water to be made easily available, (see Chapter 7 on stand pipes and bowsers).

Shelter may only be an area in shade for competitors to park their cars or trailers, but you might have to supply official show cages as at a Cat Show. Horses are expected to be on a grassed area and are usually tied to their own horse-boxes but sheep may need a pen to keep them safe and out of the crowd. Make sure that you are aware of what is expected from the organisers and supply the facilities to the highest standard that you can afford. A few extra buckets and the odd bale of straw are often useful for emergencies.

It is rare that a whole circus will be available for hire, but you may wish to employ one as part of another show or one or two circus acts by themselves. Circuses will need a certain amount of security both to keep the public out and to keep the animals in. If you can supply a fenced field or park, that helps; a grazing paddock and a safe place to exercise animals outside is even better.

VETERINARY HELP

All animals are subject to disease and accident. For large animal shows you may be required by the professional association to ensure that all animals coming to the show hold current vaccination certificates. You will need to make this clear on the schedule that will go out in advance.

It is advisable to have made a prior arrangement with a veterinary practice nearby to either have a vet available at the show itself or to have a vet on call in case of accidents. The telephone number should be given to all stewards and officials.

Just once in my time I have been present when a horse had to be shot on site. It was a most unlikely and shocking experience but one for which contingency plans had been made. The animal panicked whilst being loaded into a horse-box and broke its leg. The club had a vet on site and he examined the horse within minutes of it being injured and announced that it had to be destroyed. A horse is a large and very heavy animal and it was impossible to move it to a less public place so the deed was done there and then to prevent a curious crowd gathering, the body was covered with a tarpaulin until the ground was cleared at the end of the show and only then was it removed. In retrospect, it was felt that because the decision had been taken quickly and acted on immediately a very unfortunate incident had the minimum of publicity and the distress of the animal and it's distraught owner was kept from being prolonged. It is important to address the possibility of these potentially devastating accidents and at least decide on a plan of action or policy even if you do not go into great detail.

POSSIBLE PROBLEMS

Apart from the accident and injury problems as outlined in the above section you may experience other difficulties peculiar to animal shows.

Animal rights groups are outspoken by nature. They are also well informed and aware of all the types of animal shows in the area and if you choose to present a show that includes performing animals or circus acts you must not be surprised if they whirl into action. Whatever your own beliefs are there is, nevertheless, a growing number of the population who feel that it is wrong to allow animals the alleged indignity of performing for human beings' entertainment. Letters of a most inflammatory and infamous nature may appear in the press, pickets may hamper your ticket sales and groups bearing banners and leaflets may pervade your show ground. Is it worth it? My feeling is not, but then I confess to being on the side of the animals.

Tied into the above you may well find that council owned land is denied to you if the Local Authority has a policy of either discouraging animal acts or banning them altogether. You will need to take advice as outlined in Chapter 5.

Horse shows, in particular, are an added headache when it comes to clearing up. Your country farmer may be delighted at the offerings of fertilizer that are left, but the average park keeper will not be too thrilled. Make sure that you know what will be required of you - perhaps you could make some extra money selling bags of manure!

24 FIREWORKS AND BONFIRES

Firework and bonfire events often go together; for one the public like to get close to warm themselves and enjoy baked potatoes cooked in the embers and for the other they still like to edge closer to watch the spectacular colours and designs that modern displays can guarantee.

Fire is dangerous and can cause horrendous injuries and even prove fatal, whether in the form of a bonfire or a firework. Every year advice is given out and every year members of the public suffer dreadful accidents. They just will not be told. If you are organising a firework display or bonfire night you have to take responsibility for a generally highly irresponsible public. These shows can be more hazardous than other types of events as they are most usually held in November after sunset and often when it is cold and wet, which encourages the public to get as close as they can to the bonfire and helps cause security and car parking problems.

Pyrotechnics of all types can be arbitrary, haphazard and unreliable. Despite the growing science of firework manufacture they are still explosives contained in a case of some sort with added chemicals to provide the colours, inhibitors and

KEY POINTS

1 Never forget that fireworks can and have killed

2 If you can possibly afford it, hire the professionals

3 Choose your venue with care. Consider the firing site, the prevailing wind directions, the estimated audience numbers, what time of the evening, whether you will have other activities, crowd control and emergency procedures

4 Keep all spectators at least 40 metres from the nearest firework

5 Ensure that you have enough stewards

6 For a large display you may need a meeting with the emergency services and possibly a dummy-run of procedures

7 Have adequate first aid facilities available

8 Make sure that your public address system can be heard from all areas of the site

9 A shorter, higher display is more satisfactory and safer than a longer, ground level display. Spend your money on quality rather than quantity and keep the rate of firing up

10 Site bonfires well away from fireworks

11 Remember to inform all interested parties well in advance

12 NEVER angle a firework over the heads of spectators

bangs. Fire, in the form of a naked flame or, more commonly these days from an electrical spark, is introduced and the whole scatters across the sky in a blaze of sparks and sound. It is visually stunning and the combination of sight, sound and smell turns an ordinary night out into an exciting event tinged with a sense of danger. It is no wonder that more and more outside events and celebrations end with a finale of firework displays.

Not all firework displays take place at night and there are some pyrotechnic companies that specialise in sound shows. For some reason they have not really taken off in the UK but should you go to some countries in the Middle East and Southern Europe you will find that they are popular at all sorts of celebrations, particularly weddings and carnivals.

For a large show it is sensible to leave the actual display and firing to the experts and if you feel that you really cannot afford to bring in the professionals then, personally, I feel that you should not be holding a public display at all. However, I accept that there are situations when a group simply cannot afford to buy in a display or cope with a huge number of spectators and it is impractical to provide transport for everyone to visit a public show elsewhere. It is fun to design and organise your own show but remember, accidents happen even to those who are trained and to experienced members of well known companies.

Enough of the lecture. How do you keep a crowd safe from possible accident? You will need to think about a firing site, the wind direction, where the spectators are to watch from, crowd control and a host of other considerations. If you proceed carefully and thoroughly using all the following guide lines you will have as safe a firework display as it is possible to organise but a lot of it is down to weather conditions, the mood of the crowd and Lady Luck.

THE VENUE

In choosing a venue you will need to consider the number of spectators that you expect. It is better to choose too large a field or park than one too small where the public are pressed up against the firing site. If you decide on a public area that is served well by public transport this can go a long way towards reducing the number of cars that need to be parked and, of course, it allows families without cars the opportunity of attending.

Two firing sites should be chosen. The first allows the spectators to stand with their backs to the prevailing wind and the
second to be used in an emergency if the wind suddenly swings
round from a less predictable direction: smoke and fallout needs
to be directed away from the crowd. The firing area needs to be at
least 20 metres wide and 10 metres deep with a fall out area at the
back of at least 50 metres: (remember, casings and other debris
can travel several hundred metres in a brisk wind). It is safer to
cancel a display completely if the wind is above 30-35 mph. As a
rough guide use the rule that if debris from a test rocket or shells
blows out beyond your vision from the firing site, you should not
carry on. You should ensure that all combustible materials are
cleared and that there are no overhanging trees, long grass or
undergrowth in the area.

SPECTATORS

Before setting up the display you should already have erected the
fence that is to keep the spectators away from the fireworks.
Crowd control barriers or chestnut paling are ideal but if these are
unavailable, rope and 4 foot bumbling pins can be used, provided
a second line of rope is used about 2 foot from the ground. You
may need two or three people walking up and down the fence to
discourage the public and especially children from going round
the sides or wriggling underneath. The fence should be at least 40
metres from the nearest firework (some professional companies
insist on 100m, but for small material such is available to the
amateur market 40m should be adequate), and you should not
allow anybody, even the firing team, to enter the fall out area to the
rear of the display.

STAFF AND STEWARDS

You will need as many helpers as you can muster and they should
be easily identified. Fluorescent waistcoats are ideal. The recommended minimum number of stewards is two for the first 50
spectators and one for each additional 250. Prior to the show you
should make arrangements with the Police and/or the Fire Brigade about how best to evacuate the spectators and get emergency vehicles on to the site; each steward should know these
procedures plus the layout of the site and the running order. For
a large display it may be necessary to have some stewards in radio

contact with the firing team and the emergency crew.

You will need additional staff to supervise the bonfire if there is one and the exits and entrances. The latter should be well observed to ensure that the general public do not bring their own fireworks onto the site; this should be well publicised in advance both on the posters and again on signs at each entrance. There should be enough gates to facilitate evacuation should it become necessary.

FIRE FIGHTING

Allocate special duties to two or three of your stewards to provide a fire fighting team. They should have an adequate number of fire extinguishers and supplies of sand and water. It is prudent to provide training (the Fire Services can advise on this subject) in advance for the use of extinguishers and other fire fighting equipment.

FIRST AID

The Red Cross or St. John Ambulance Brigade should be invited to attend for half an hour before and during the whole display and remain until the site is cleared.

Although an independent first aid team should be available it is sensible to provide a fairly extensive first aid kit yourselves. Include a roll of cling film in the kit as it makes a perfect sterile, non-stick (to the surface of wounds) protection for burns until they can be treated in a more conventional way. Clean burns, cuts and grazes well, using only clean water and - excluding the face - wrap gently in the film and wait for medical assistance.

PUBLIC ADDRESS

A public address system should be used at larger displays whereas a hand held loudhailer or megaphone should be adequate for small shows. Make sure that all sections of the crowd can hear the PA as it may be vital if evacuation becomes necessary.

THE DISPLAY

Various factors will determine the choice of fireworks. Budget will be a large consideration and if money is tight today's sophisticated crowds far prefer a short but spectacular show, fired in quick succession than a long traditional display firing each firework one at a time.

Crowds far prefer a short but spectacular show, fired in quick succession.

112

Even if money is no object (and there cannot be many displays where the organisers are not carefully counting each penny), about 20 minutes is enough for an exciting and noisy display. It is uncomfortable standing in the cold looking up at the sky and being bombarded by loud explosions and after a while even the keenest firework enthusiast looks forward to the end.

There are really only five groups of fireworks and your site will determine the combination and types used. First, there are the well known aerial shells which come in a variety of sizes ranging from 1 1/2" - 14" and are launched from a mortar buried in the ground; they travel hundreds of feet into the sky and explode at the peak of the flight. Second are the type known as candles and include the favourite Roman Candles, these consist of multishock tubes of material that provide an effect lasting 30-40 seconds. Third are rockets fired from a stick and known to all from our childhoods when most of us bought a 'special' rocket from the corner shop to fire from a milk bottle. They have come on a great deal since the fifties and sixties and can be a very exciting addition to any show. Fourth are mines which like shells are fired from mortars. These explode straight out of the tube and push up stars and plumes of coloured smoke to about 15'. And lastly there are the set pieces which consist of Catherine Wheels, fireworks attached to poles, frames or lettering. These are often used to start or finish a show or to advertise a sponsor.

The best fireworks to use if your site is flat and level are the high firing aerial shells or rockets so that all spectators can have an optimum view. On an elevated firing area you can get away with ground level fireworks and use the frames mentioned above to include messages or pictures into your display. Mines should also be restricted to elevated sites.

Try to keep your firing team to a minimum and ideally they should have had some experience. Each operator should have a particular section or job allocated and the whole team should rehearse the show (using dummies, naturally) to familiarise themselves with the running order, the instructions and the fireworks themselves a couple of days in advance. If there is anything that they are not sure about you will have time to telephone the suppliers.

All high firing fireworks should be angled over the fall out area and well away from the spectators so that the spent cases and materials land where they can do least damage. Fall out can also cause serious damage to paint work so make sure the car park is well away from the site or you could find yourselves with an insurance claim.

Read the instructions that are printed by law on every firework and obey them to the letter; it is easy to put a shell upside-down into a mortar and having lit the fuse it can only explode underground scattering hot debris at a horrifying rate over everybody within range. All fireworks that are released for sale to the public have to include a 5-8 second delay. This is a British standard and you have a right to complain of any material that fails to give you this provision.

BONFIRES

Make sure that any bonfire is sited well away from the firing area and always down wind so that sparks cannot accidentally ignite the display. Ideally it should be well fenced off using metal interlocking crowd control barriers and continuously supervised. Check the bonfire carefully for animals, aerosols, cans of paint, tyres or anything hazardous before it is lit: there have also been cases of children making dens in unlit bonfires, which may have been there for days. And ensure that it is completely extinguished before you leave the site.

Unless you are holding a private display in your garden it is extremely unwise to cook anything in the embers. A large bonfire gives off a tremendous heat and takes a very long time to cool down; few people can be bothered to wait until the coals are safe enough for cooking.

INFORMING THE AUTHORITIES

The Police, the Fire Brigade and the Ambulance Services all need to know where the display is being held, the date and time and which access will be used. If an airport is near the site you should inform them of your display if it is a large one, and it is a courtesy to notify hospitals, sheltered housing, animal sanctuaries, farmers or any other nearby residents if you think they may be affected.

25 A WORD ABOUT FOOD

Good and varied food can be a very attractive part of most events and there is usually one way or another that you can choose the food to fit your theme, be it Elizabethan apple pastries for an Early Dance Exhibition, food from around the world for an ethnic cultures trade festival, vegetarian for a Green Fair, or a full scale Medieval Banquet. Even the local fete would be lost without the traditional WI stall to offer its delicious supplies of fresh cakes, breads and home bottled jams and pickles.

But the inclusion of food can be a real problem. Where to keep it until it is wanted? How to keep it cool? How to keep it hot? What to do with the left overs? How to gauge the demand correctly? What to do with the dirty dishes? Where to prepare it in the first place? But above all: how to keep food safe to eat?

In the following sections I hope to improve your knowledge, or remind you, of the good hygiene practises that you should use and the regulations that cover the provision of food at events and shows. (By 'food' I mean both food and drink throughout the chapter.) It may not be such a problem if you are holding

KEY POINTS

1. Do not be put off including food within your event as it can be a vital attraction, but make sure your committee is fully aware of all the legal requirements

2. If you are at all concerned or confused ALWAYS talk to your local Environmental Health Department or Trading Standards Office well in advance

3. If someone is regularly preparing food for public consumption it would be sensible to suggest they take a Basic Food Hygiene Certificate Course

4. Remember that it is not only food offered for sale that is subject to the Food Safety Laws, it covers a lot of produce offered to the public whether money changes hands or not

5. Be aware of the very high risk foods and be especially careful

6. New temperature controls come into use from April 1993: the details will be available from your local Council

7. It is unlikely that you will have to register with the local authority, but it is as well to check that your organisation is exempt if you are unsure

8. Make sure that barbecues are used correctly

9. Ensure that your group is aware of the laws surrounding food labelling and make yourselves familiar with the policies in practice in your area. Take advice if necessary

10. Use the golden rules of food safety

your event indoors, especially if you have access to a purpose built kitchen that includes sinks, a fridge and a good food preparation area that has recently been inspected by an Environmental Health Officer. Of course you should still use safe preparation techniques as outlined in the Ten Golden Rules below but basic facilities such as 'fridges, separate sinks and easily cleaned surfaces should all be available.

Outdoors it is a different matter altogether. Most events take place in the Summer at a time when we all hope that it will be warm and sunny, in fact perfect weather for breeding dangerous bacteria, so caterers will have to be especially vigilant.

EXEMPTIONS FROM REGULATIONS

You will have to make up your mind whether the service you are providing could be described as a business. In the terms of the regulations covering aspects of food handling the word 'business' is extended to include "the undertaking of a canteen, club, school, hospital or institution, whether carried on for profit or not". In these cases the organisers of any event will clearly have to comply with the regulations detailed later in the chapter. However, in many cases voluntary organisations will not need to comply and to give an example from the bottom end of the spectrum, if you were to throw a party for your friends but asked for £2.00 to help pay for the food no enforcing authority would care two hoots. But, when you get into the realms of taking a stall on the local market to sell your cakes for profit, even if that profit is for charity, then your activities may be viewed in a very different way. In general the more commercial your operation appears to be, especially if you are acting in competition with traders, the more likely it is that the relevant authorities will be interested. If you are providing food at a very low key event such as at a Church Fete, officers are only likely to show interest if there is illness as a result of a hygiene problem.

The thing to remember is that many of the relevant regulations are fairly new and there are very few cases to test the legislation against. Whilst specific areas, such as canteens, schools etc. have been specified it is still not absolutely clear that food and drink supplied at other charity or fundraising events is covered, even if it is charged for, and we may have to wait a few years for a case or two to come to court and clarify the law. It is, as the legal people say 'a grey area'!. What is undeniable is that you should try to comply with the regulations anyway since they exist to promote hygiene and safety.

REGISTRATION

As from 1991 all food premises and mobile food vehicles operating as a business, now have to register with the Local Authority which covers the area of the premises or, in the case of a vehicle, where it is garaged at night. If you are selling pitches for food vans it helps to ask for payment in advance (see Chapter 6 under the section on Pricing); at this stage you can compile a list and check for registration yourself or send the list to the Council if your event is held on Council owned land. Remember, the person who has control of the premises being used for a food business or the land where stalls and vehicles are parked has a legal duty to take all reasonable steps to ensure that the hygiene regulations are being observed. If the 'organiser/manager' has taken no reasonable steps to ensure compliance, s/he could also face prosecution under the Food Hygiene Regulations even if the event itself is not a 'food business'.

Usually, if your committee is organising the provision of food on a one-off basis you do not have to register; however you should still observe good hygiene practices. If you are selling food over a period of days you may be required to register unless you are covered by the exemptions detailed below and you should take advice from your Local Authority. There are certain food premises, stands, stalls, vehicles etc. that are exempt from the requirement to register.

First, registration only applies to food premises. Second, it does not apply to the supply of beverages, biscuits, potato crisps, confectionery or other similar products ancillary to a business which is not the sale of food.

Third, it does not apply to premises controlled by a voluntary organisation or the trustees of a charity which are used only for their own purposes and where no food (other than dry ingredients for the preparation of refreshments such as tea, coffee, sugar, biscuits, crisps and other similar dry products) is stored for sale.

And fourth, where the premises are domestic premises but the proprietor of the business does not live there. By this you can suppose that the proprietor of the business might be the voluntary organisation itself, in which case a member of that organisation may well be able to prepare food at home without registration.

FOOD HYGIENE

I shall try to include a few guidelines for safe food preparation, but anyone who is to work with food to any great extent would be well advised to study the Basic Food Hygiene Certificate course that will be available in your area. The Basic Certificate normally takes six hours tuition and the qualification is recognised nationally. Display your certificate with pride, on your stall and suggest that any regular helpers (or staff) also have the certificate.

Although exact requirements have yet to be agreed, the Government does have powers under the Food Safety Act to introduce compulsory food hygiene training for those involved in food businesses. This gives you some idea of the amount of importance that is attached to proper training in areas of food preparation, transport and storage.

If you are a member of the WI you may be able to obtain training through the Institute itself as they have their own tutors. Annual refresher training is recommended because hygiene regulations often change. Two excellent publications to give you information in greater detail are 'Guidelines for the Catering Industry on the Food Hygiene (Amendment) Regulations 1990 and 1991' from the Department of Health and 'Essentials of Health and Safety at Work' from the Health and Safety Executive; both books are available from any HMSO bookstore and addresses are given at the back of the book.

A large part of food safety is common sense but there are regulations which have been tightened in recent years and, in ignorance, you could run the risk of prosecution. Unlike other areas of law, food safety is all about being able to prove that you are within the law, for example, if an inspector finds unfit food on your stall, how can you prove your innocence? How can an inspector tell if an un-refrigerated sandwich was made legally within the last four hours? Of course s/he can't, unless it is a follow up visit and s/he actually saw you making the last batch within so many hours. But if you have kept records making it clear when each batch and type were put together you will be more likely to be believed.

If you have any concerns at all it is prudent to talk to your Local Authority's Health Department well in advance of any event and they will be very happy to advise you.

TEN GOLDEN RULES FOR FOOD HYGIENE

1. **ALWAYS** wash your hands before handling food and after going to the toilet.

2. **TELL** your boss, or supervisor, at once of any skin, nose, throat or bowel trouble.

3. **ENSURE** cuts and sores are covered with waterproof dressings (preferably blue).

4. **KEEP** yourself clean and wear clean clothing.

5. **DO NOT SMOKE** in a food room. It is illegal and dangerous. Never cough or sneeze over food.

6. **CLEAN** as you go. Keep all equipment and surfaces clean.

7. **PREPARE** raw and cooked food in separate areas. Keep food covered and either refrigerated or piping hot.

8. **KEEP** your hands off food as far as possible.

9. **ENSURE** waste food is disposed of properly. Keep the lid on the dustbin and wash your hands after putting waste in it.

10. **TELL** your supervisor if you cannot follow the rules.
    DO NOT BREAK THE LAW

(information provided by Food Sense booklet No.PB0351)

BARBECUES

This form of catering is the Environmental Health Officer's nightmare. Food is often prepared by amateur chefs - frequently someone who does not even cook on a regular basis. People underestimate the length of time that the barbecue should be alight before food is cooked on it, grills and utensils are often dirty and the food can be horribly underdone. This type of cooking uses hot coals and naked flames and can also be dangerous. There have been serious accidents involving barbecues being blown or knocked over.

In its favour, correctly barbecued food is a delicious form of outside catering and because you often cook to order it is a good way to judge supply and demand. You are not restricted to meat or even savoury foods. There are many vegetarian foods that you can barbecue, especially when wrapped in foil and some fruits are particularly good cooked in this way or as kebabs.

Don't forget to have the area well lit if you are cooking at night. It is hard to tell in the dark if food is cooked adequately.

SIMPLE GUIDELINES FOR BARBECUES

1. Use clean utensils and equipment
2. Make sure that you wash them frequently and that you have separate facilities for washing hands
3. You need an adequate supply of hot and cold water
4. A thermometer is recommended to check the temperatures of cooked food
5. Make sure that your barbecue is really hot. Ideally you should light the charcoal 1 hour before you use it. After 20 minutes rake the embers into an even layer, cover with more charcoal and leave for another 30-40 minutes to ensure there are no cold spots
6. Keep all raw food as cool as possible and eat cooked food as soon as it is ready
7. Ensure that food is thoroughly cooked all through, use thin cuts where possible
8. As soon as you finish cooking remove the grills to prevent grease from becoming burnt on
9. Do not transport the barbecue until it is absolutely cold
10. Always follow the Golden Rules for food hygiene as outlined in this chapter

PICNIC AREAS

This is a great way out of having to provide food. Suggest that people bring their own. You could, of course, provide a picnic area anyway for the take-away food provided on site. The advantages are that you can control the litter and restrict food being taken into exhibition areas.

Any grassy space away from traffic or animals and adequately roped off would be suitable. Provide lots of bins and a few tables and chairs and let the public do the rest.

FOOD SAFETY ACT, 1990

This Act goes slightly wider than the regulations discussed above and covers all food; not just that prepared from a business premises. Local Government Inspectors now have greater powers than ever and are quite within their rights to inspect any premises making or preparing food for the general public. The Food Safety Act, 1990 governs the condition of the food itself. If you are found to be offering unfit food for sale or your food is falsely or misleadingly labelled you could be fined a maximum of £20,000 and/or imprisoned. So you need to be aware of where you might be contravening the law. Unfit food could include food that is infected with bacteria or that includes foreign bodies - anything from insect larvae to nails. Some foods are more likely to grow food poisoning organisms than others and particular care should be taken when preparing meat, fish, dairy products and pastries or cakes including fresh cream, egg dishes and cooked rice.

It is as well to realise that this regulation is exceptional in that it covers any food that is not safe even when there is no business element. If the supply is part of a business then the regulation applies even if the food is free. It also applies to anything that might be prepared for prizes or even given away to the general public at a social gathering of almost any kind. An Environmental Health Officer is entitled to inspect any premises if he suspects that an offence has been committed, including a domestic kitchen. This would almost certainly only happen if s/he had been alerted to a possible problem by a complaint about say, a piece of glass being found in the middle of a homemade cake. However, in the case of domestic premises officers are not permitted to make an inspection (except with a magistrates warrant) unless 24 hours notice in writing has been given. At the very worst, the cook could find herself prosecuted under the Food Safety Act for the foreign body and under the Hygiene Regulations for having a kitchen that was below the recommended standard. In practice this is highly unlikely to happen unless the complaint was very serious.

FOOD HYGIENE (General) REGULATIONS, 1970 AS AMENDED

If your operation is not classified as a business ('business' meaning the extended definition as discussed at the beginning of this chapter under 'Exemptions') you will not be covered by the above regulations. However any outside caterers or mobile food vans that you might employ all have to comply. If you are not happy that they are carrying out their business properly then you can complain to your Environmental Health Department.

This law covers permanent premises, equipment and food handlers associated with the preparation of food for consumption by the general public within a food business. It also includes all stages of that process including transportation, storage, packaging and even the seller of the food if that person comes into direct contact with the products.

The 'amended' part of the Law covers the new temperature regulations and you can learn more about these from the leaflet 'Stay Safe -FH1/E' which should be available from your local

Environmental Health Department or from the Health Publications Unit (address at the back of the book). In April 1993 even more rigorous temperature control will be enforced; these are also covered in the 'Stay Safe' leaflet.

THE FOOD HYGIENE (Markets, Stalls and Delivery vehicles) REGULATIONS, 1966 AS AMENDED

These regulations cover the types of food businesses (again this means the extended definition) that you are likely to find at outside events and include the hygiene and temperature requirements and question of registration which match those set out in the sections above.

The law applies to stands, marquees and tents, mobile canteens, vending machines or any site or pitch from which food is provided. It is probably thought not to be relevant to stalls or stands that are selling items made by volunteers as a means of raising funds for another organisation. But you should be aware of the requirements and, again as above, if you are not happy with the commercial operation that you bought in or rented a pitch to, you can complain.

FOOD LABELLING

It is very hard to pin any of the professionals down on this subject. They know what the law states and as far as commercial companies are concerned they are prepared to follow it to the letter and throw the book at anyone who looks like behaving outside the law. But, and I think this is because of the 'it has always been so' factor involved, small fetes, WI stalls, charity stands in the Church hall and the produce left for auction after a Garden Produce and Horticultural Show tends to be treated rather more leniently in practice if not in theory. But you will not find any Trading Standards Officer anywhere in the country admitting this.

In many cases the food labelling requirements will not apply due to exemptions which cover prepared meals, sandwiches, and un-packaged food. However, and I am sticking my neck out here, even where labelling might be considered necessary, I honestly do not believe that any inspector is going to prosecute if food offered for sale is not labelled absolutely correctly as long as it has been prepared hygienically and with a responsible attitude towards preparation and storage and is offered for sale within a reasonable period suitably protected with a wrapper or other container.

Of course, if there were complaints the manufacturer may still be liable under the Food Safety Act as shown in the example at the beginning of this chapter. One of the requirements is to state the producer's name and address on each product and if this was missing from an item which was the subject of a complaint your organising group might find themselves the target for prosecution in the absence or proof of the true perpetrator.

In the light of this responsibility you might consider insisting that you accept no food product for sale that does not bear the name and address of the person who made it. On the other hand there is a very real danger of putting genuine volunteer cooks off the idea of producing food if it all has to carry their name and address. Perhaps a way round this understandable stumbling block is to keep a record of all items and their manufacturers. You would then be able to trace produce back to source if there was a complaint.

LABELLING PRODUCE

The strict letter of the law insists that the following information is stated on a label attached to each product:

1. The name of the food (which must not be misrepresented in any way)
2. Description of what it is, if not covered by 1.
3. Name and address of manufacturer
4. 'Best before date' or 'Use by date'
5. Any specific storage instructions
6. List of ingredients starting with the greatest first by weight and including any additives

If you follow the above rules you will be seen to doing all you possibly can to conform, although just the first three instructions should be enough to cover most low-risk foods. Some other products must list specific percentages e.g. Cooked meat products and jams must list the amount of meat and fruit respectively.

USEFUL PUBLICATIONS

 IDEAS

**ENGINEERS OF THE IMAGINATION –
THE WELFARE STATE HANDBOOK**
Edited by Tony Coult and Baz Kershaw, published by Methuen London Ltd, 11 New Fetter Lane, London EC4 4EE. Price £8.99

FUNDRAISING CAN BE FUN RAISING
Great Ormond Street Children's Hospital Fundraising package. *Available free of charge from Great Ormond Street Hospital.*

THE COMPLETE FUNDRAISING HANDBOOK
by Sam Clarke, published by the Directory of Social Change, Radius Works, Back Lane, London, NW3 1HL Tel:(071) 435 8171 Price £9.95

HOW TO RAISE FUNDS AND SPONSORSHIP
by Chriss McCallum, published by How To Books, Plymbridge House, Estover Road, Plymouth PL6 7PZ. Price £7.99

 COMMITTEES AND ORGANISING GROUPS

GETTING ORGANISED
by Christine Holloway and Shirely Otto, published by the National Council of Voluntary Organisations, available from the Directory of Social Change, Radius Works, Back Lane, London, NW3 1HL Tel:(071) 435 8171. Price £5.95

STARTING AND RUNNING A VOLUNTARY GROUP
by Sally Capper, Judith Unell and Anne Weyman published by the National Council of Voluntary Organisations, available from the Directory of Social Change, Radius Works, Back Lane, London, NW3 1HL Tel:(071) 435 8171. Price £3.95

VOLUNTARY BUT NOT AMATEUR
by Duncan Forbes, Ruth Hayes and Jacki Reason published by the London Voluntary Services Council, available from the Directory of Social Change, Radius Works, Back Lane, London, NW3 1HL Tel:(071) 435 8171. Price £7.95

JUST ABOUT MANAGING

by Sandy Merritt Adirondack published by the London Voluntary Service Council, available from the Directory of Social Change, Radius Works, Back Lane, London, NW3 1HL Tel:(071) 435 8171. Price £10.95

THE MANAGEMENT OF VOLUNTARY ORGANISATIONS

published by Croner Publications Ltd. Croner House, London Road, Kingston-upon-Thames, Surrey, KT2 6SR. Tel:(081) 547 3333. *This is a very large, loose-leaf for easy update, publication and due to its rather high cost probably best looked for in a library. It is well worth studying on all sorts of topics.*

THE DIRECTORY OF VOLUNTEERING AND EMPLOYMENT OPPORTUNITIES WITH CHARITIES

available in March 1993 from the Directory of Social Change, Radius Works, Back Lane, London, NW3 1HL Tel:(071) 435 8171. Price £7.95. *A publication on volunteers.*

▌ PROFESSIONAL ENTERTAINERS, ACTS AND SERVICES

SHOWCALL DIRECTORY

compiled and published by the Stage and Television Today, 47 Bermondsey Street, London, SE1 3XT Tel:(071) 403 1818. Price £18.00

THE SHOWMAN'S DIRECTORY

compiled and published by Lance Publications, Brook House, Mint Street, Godalming, Surrey GU7 1HE Tel.(0483) 422184. Price £17.00

▌ PUBLICITY AND MARKETING

GUIDE TO ARTS MARKETING

by Keith Diggle, published by Rhinegold Publishing Ltd, 52a Floral Street, London, WC2E 9DA Tel:(071) 836 2534. *This book is now out of print but you may be able to find it in a library.*

MARKETING: A HANDBOOK FOR CHARITIES

by Dorothy and Alistair McIntosh published by the Directory of Social Change, Radius Works, Back Lane, London, NW3 1HL Tel:(071) 435 8171. Price £7.95

A BASIC PR GUIDE

by Dorothy and Alistair McIntosh , published by the Directory of Social Change, Radius Works, Back Lane, London, NW3 1HL Tel:(071) 435 8171 Price £4.50

THE THEORY AND PRACTICE OF THEATRE MARKETING

edited by Glyn V. Robbins and Peter Verwey, published by the Theatrical Management Association, available from John Offord Publications, 12, The Avenue, Eastbourne, East Sussex BN21 3AY Tel:(0323) 37841. Price not available.

 VOLUNTEERS

THE VOLUNTARY AGENCIES DIRECTORY

compiled and published by the National Council of Voluntary Organisations, available from the Directory of Social Change, Radius Works, Back Lane, London, NW3 1HL Tel:(071) 435 8171 Price £10.95

SPONSORSHIP AND FUNDRAISING

ASSOCIATION FOR BUSINESS SPONSORSHIP OF THE ARTS / W H SMITH SPONSORSHIP MANUAL

available through W.H.S. Smith stores.

A GUIDE TO THE MAJOR TRUSTS

1993 edition published by the Directory of Social Change, Radius Works, Back Lane, London, NW3 1HL Tel:(071) 435 8171. Price £14.95

A GUIDE TO COMPANY GIVING

1993 edition, edited by Michael and Nicola Eastwood, published by the Directory of Social Change, Radius Works, Back Lane, London, NW3 1HL Tel:(071) 435 8171. Price £14.95

THE MAJOR COMPANIES GUIDE
edited by David Casson, published by the Directory of Social Change, Radius Works, Back Lane, London, NW3 1HL Tel:(071) 435 8171. Price £14.95

THE LONDON GRANTS GUIDE
edited by Nicola Parker and John Stephen, published by the Directory of Social Change, Radius Works, Back Lane, London, NW3 1HL Tel:(071) 435 8171. Price £12.50

WEST MIDLANDS GRANTS GUIDE
edited by Nicola Eastwood and Daren Felgate, published by the Directory of Social Change, Radius Works, Back Lane, London, NW3 1HL Tel:(071) 435 8171. Price £9.95

EXPLAINING THE LAW
(Most of the Government publications are free of charge and should be available from your local council.)

PRACTICAL LAW FOR ARTS ADMINISTRATORS
by Charles Arnold-Baker published by John Offord (Publications) Ltd. PO Box 64, Eastbourne, East Sussex Tel:(0323) 37841. Price not available.

'AND JUDY WILL RUN THE CAKE STALL'
available free of charge with a SAE from Parkinson Cowen Brochure Services, 636 Bristol Road South, Birmingham, B31 2JR

THE FOOD SAFETY ACT, 1990 AND YOU –
A GUIDE FOR THE FOOD INDUSTRY
published by H.M.Government, available from Food Sense, London SE99 7TT Tel:(081) 694 8862

GUIDELINES FOR THE CATERING INDUSTRY ON
THE FOOD HYGIENE (Amendment) REGULATIONS
1990 AND 1991
published by the Department of Health, available from HMSO Bookshops

THE FOOD HYGIENE (Markets, Stalls and Delivery Vehicles) REGULATIONS 1966 AS AMENDED BY THE FOOD HYGIENE (Amendment) REGULATIONS 1990
published by Eaton Publications, P.O. Box 34, Walton-on-Thames, Surrey, Tel:(0932) 229001

ESSENTIALS OF HEALTH AND SAFETY AT WORK
published by the Health and Safety Executive, available from HMSO Bookshops

LOTTERIES AND AMUSEMENTS ACT, 1976
Cat No. BL5, published by Shaw and Sons Ltd, Shaway House, Lower Syndham, SE26 5AE

GUIDE TO HEALTH, SAFETY AND WELFARE AT POP CONCERTS AND OTHER SIMILAR EVENTS
available from the Health and Safety Executive, Baynards House, 1 Chepstow Place, London W2 4TF

VAT LEAFLET 701/1/92
available from H.M. Customs and Excise Office

RECREATION AND THE LAW
by Valerie Collins, published by E & F N Spon, 11 New Fetter Lane, London EC4P 4EE. Price £13.95

 **SPECIAL NEEDS**

both participatory or as audience

THE CREATIVE TREE
edited by Gina Levete, published by Michael Russell (Publishing) Ltd, The Chantry, Wilton, Salisbury, Wiltshire. Price £7.95

ARTS FOR EVERYONE
by Anne Pearson, published by the Carnegie Trust, available from Centre on Environment for the Handicapped, 126 Albert Street, London NW1 7NF. Price £ 6.00

📖 FIREWORK DISPLAYS

GUIDELINES FOR ORGANISERS OF PROFESSIONALLY FIRED FIREWORK DISPLAYS
compiled and published by the British Pyrotechnists' Association, available free of charge from 1, Hill View Road, Hatch End, Pinner, Middlesex, HA5 4PB

FIREWORK FACT SHEET
complied by the Firework Makers Guild, available free of charge from Health and Safety Offices and local Fire Services

📖 SCIENCE OF LEISURE AND ORGANISING

THE SOCIOLOGY OF LEISURE
by S. Parker, published by Allen and Unwin, London. *Out of print now but available in libraries.*

ORGANISATION THEORY
edited by D.S.Pugh, published by Penguin Books Ltd, Harmondsworth, Middlesex. Price £8.99

USEFUL ADDRESSES

 IDEAS

British Film Institute
21 Stephen Street,
London W1P 1PL
Tel: 071 255 1444
May help find films to show

**Royal Scottish Country
Dance Society**
12 Coates Crescent,
Edinburgh, Scotland EH3 7AF
Tel: 031 225 3854
May help find your local group

**Association of Circus
Proprietors of Great Britain**
Malcolm Clay, Secretary,
25-29 Victoria Street,
Blackburn, Lancs, BB1 6DN
Tel: (0254 67) 2222
*Can advise and assist finding
reputable circuses and acts*

Peeks of Bournmouth Ltd
Riverside Lane,
Tuckton, Christchurch,
Bournemouth, Dorset BH6 3LD
Tel: (0202) 4177777
*Complete fundraising packages
including games, novelties,
Balloons, etc.*

Wall's Carnival Stores Ltd
155/161 Caversham Road,
Reading, Berkshire RG1 8BB
Tel: (0734) 586727
*Fundraising packages, as above -
also balloon gas*

Carousel Fun Fairs Agency
Plot 24, The Plantation,
West Park Road,
Newchapel, Surrey RH7 6HT
Tel: (0342) 717707
*Dozens of fairground
entertainments to hire
and book*

 VENUES

If you have set your heart on an
historical monument to site your
event you can try your luck with
the following

English Heritage
Fortress House,
23 Savile Row, London W1
Tel: 071 973 3000

Historic Scotland
20 Brandon Street,
Edinburgh, Scotland EH3 5RA
Tel: 031 244 3144

**Cadw Welsh Historic
Monuments**
9th Floor,
Brunel House,
2 Fitzalan Road,
Cardiff, Wales CF2 1UY
Tel: (0222) 465511

REGULATIONS

**Gaming Board of
Great Britain**
Berkshire House,
168-173 High Holborn,
London WC1V 7AA
Tel: 071 240 0821
*Advice and registration for all
forms of lotteries where prizes
are offered over £2,000*

Customs and Excise
New Kings Beam House,
22 Upper Ground,
London SE1 9PJ
Tel: 071 620 1313
*Advice on VAT or your
local office*

**The Performing Rights
Society Ltd**
29-33 Berners Street,
London W1P 4AA
Tel: 071 580 5544
*Advice on fees that may
be payable for live music.*

INFRASTRUCTURE

RAC Signs Service
RAC House,
M1 Cross, Brent Terrace,
London NW2 1LT
Tel: 0800 234810 (Freephone)
*Highway signs and planning
permission*

AA Signs Service
Fanum House,
Dogkennel Lane,
Halesowen, West Midlands B63 3BT
Tel: 021 501
*Highway signs and planning
permission*

GKN Quickform (Birmingham)
Tel: 021 7063399 for your
nearest office
*Crowd control barriers
and fencing*

SGB Readyfence
Tel: 081 628 3400 for your
nearest office
All types of temporary fencing

**The Amazing Bunting
Company**
PO Box 274,
Northampton NN3 4AD
Tel: 0604 786655
*as stated, bunting and other
types of bazaar and fair
equipment*

**Restroom Rentals /
The Search Group**
Tel: 0532 639081 for your
nearest office
Lavatories

Pilot Hire Ltd
Wimpey Estate, Lancaster Road,
Southall, Middlesex UB1 1NR
Tel: 081 574 3882
*Lavatories including disabled
facilities*

Nipperbout
84 Clonmell Road,
London N17 6JU
Tel: 081 801 0148
Mobile creche / childcare

 PUBLICITY

Ticketshop
13, Cremyll Road,
Reading, Berkshire RG1 8NQ
Tel: 0734 599234
Official tickets and publicity

Geerings of Ashford Ltd
Cobbs Wood House,
Chart Road,
Ashford, Kent TN23 1EP
Tel: 0233 633366
Full publicity service including catalogues and schedules

 A FEW FUNDING SOURCES

Arts Council of Great Britain
14 Great Peter Street,
London SW1P 3NQ
Tel: 071 333 0100

Arts Council of Northern Ireland
185 Stranmillis Road,
Belfast, Northern Ireland BT9 5DU
Tel: 0232 381591

Crafts Council
44a Pentonville Road,
Islington, London N1 9BY
Tel: 071 278 7700

Gulbenkian Foundation
98 Portland Place,
London W1N 4ET
Tel: 071 636 5313

London Chamber of Commerce and Industry
69 Cannon Street,
London EC4N 5AB
Tel: 071 248 4444

 FIREWORKS

Shell Shock Fireworks Company
South Manor farm,
Bramfield,
Halesworth, Suffolk IP19 9AQ
Tel: 0986 84469
Importers and designers of high tech firework and laser shows

Standard Fireworks
Standard Drive,
Crosland Hill,
Huddersfield HD4 7AD
Tel: 0484 640640
Manufacturers and designers of firework displays

Kimbolton Fireworks
7 High Street,
Kimbolton, Cambs PE18 0HB
Tel: 0480 860988
Manufacturers and designers of firework displays

⌂ MISCELLANEOUS

BBC
Broadcasting House,
Portland Place,
London W1A 1AA
Tel: 071 580 4468

Independent Television Commission
70 Brompton Road,
London SW3 1EY
Tel: 071 584 7011

ILAM (Institute of Leisure and Amenity Management)
ILAM House,
Lower Basildon,
Reading, Berks RG8 9NE
Tel: 0491 874222
May help if you have a dispute with your local council's Recreation Department

Central Register of Charities
St. Alban's House,
57/60 Haymarket,
London SW1Y 4QX
Tel: 071 210 3000
Register of all charities

Charity Commission
St Alban's House,
57/60 Haymarket,
London SW1Y 4QX
Tel: 071 210 4405
Advice and numerous leaflets on all charitable concerns

Charities Aid Foundation
48 Pembury Road,
Tonbridge, Kent TN9 2JD
Tel: (07327) 713333
More charity advice

Companies Registry, England
Companies House,
Crown Way,
Maindy, Cardiff, Wales CF4 3UZ
Tel: (0222) 388588

Companies Registry, Scotland
Companies House,
102 George Street,
Edinburgh, Scotland EH2 3DG
Tel: 031 225 5774

National Federation of Women's Institutes
104 New King's Road,
London SW6 4LY
Tel: 071 371 9300
Information on local groups

The National Outdoor Events Association
7 Hamilton Way,
Wallington, Surrey SM6 9NJ
Tel: 081 669 8121
May help with all aspects of events, especially large shows. Sort of entertainments business watchdog.

SPECIMEN CHECKLIST

EVENT: DATE: TIME:

VENUE:

ADMISSION:

CAR PARK: CHARGE:

EVENT HQ:

CONTACT:

ADDRESS: TEL:

HIRE FEE: DEPOSIT:

ACTS / ENTERTAINMENT:

PAYGATE / FENCING:

CHANGING ROOMS:

MARQUEE:

CHAIRS / TABLES:

TOILETS:

OTHER EQUIPMENT:

CATERING:

LICENSEE:

WATER:

ELECTRICITY:

LIGHTING:

CONCESSIONS:

RAFFLE:

REFUSE:

SOUND SYSTEM / PA:

VEHICLE ACCESS:

CHILDREN:

SPECIAL REQUIREMENTS:

FLOWERS:

PUBLIC LIABILITY INSURANCE:

OTHER INSURANCE:

FIRE PREVENTION:

SAFETY CERTIFICATES:

POLICE NOTIFICATION:

POLICE / SECURITY:

FIRST AID:

POSTERS / PUBLICITY:

RADIO:

SIGNING:

SPECIAL APPROVALS:

ENTERTAINMENTS LICENCE:

LIQUOR LICENCE:

COLLECTION LICENCE:

LOTTERIES LICENCE:

CASH SECURITY / COLLECTION:

FLOAT MONEY / WAGES:

STEWARDS:

CIVIC DIGNITARIES:

BOUQUET:

SPECIAL ARRANGEMENTS:

NOTES:

SPECIMEN MARKETING CHECKLIST

EVENT: DATE: TIMES:

VENUE:

ADDRESS:

ADMISSION:

TEL NO. OF CONTACT:

SPONSORS:

BENEFITING CHARITY:

PRESS RELEASE 1*:

PRESS RELEASE 2*:

PRESS RELEASE 3*:

POSTERS:

LEAFLETS:

TICKETS:

PROMOTIONS:

EVENT STATIONARY:

PROGRAMME:

Press release to be sent out, for example, 6 weeks prior, 1 week prior, and when anything significant has been achieved.

SITE PLAN:

CATALOGUE:

SCHEDULE:

COMPETITION:

PRESS ADS:

OTHER ADS:

FREEBIES:

BADGES:

DISPLAY/EXHIBITION:

PRE-EVENT EVENT:

LAUNCH:

RECEPTION:

THANK YOU PARTY:

NOTES